BRITAIN'S CASTLES

Susie Hodge

This first edition published in Great Britain in 2012 by
Crimson Publishing Ltd
Westminster House
Kew Road
Richmond
Surrey
TW9 2ND

© Crimson Publishing Ltd, 2012

The right of Susie Hodge to be identified as the author of this work has been asserted by her in accordance with the
Copyright, Designs and Patents Act, 1988.

ISBN 978 1 78059 076 9

Designed and typeset by Michael King

Printed and bound by Craft Print, Singapore

PICTURE CREDITS

Photographs are reproduced with the permission of the following:

Bill McKenzie BM photo: p.85; p.86
Corbis, © Jason Hawkes: p.21
David Mitchell (Flickr): p. 8 top centre; p.28
Dreamstime.com, © Fonetix: p.5; p.63; © Alfiofer: p.11; © Dennis Dolkens: p.88; ©CharlieW75: p.22;
© Tonyd p.37; © Gail Johnson: p.42; p.53; p.60; © Emeraldgreen: p.49
istock: p.6 top left, top right, centre, bottom left; p.7 bottom right; p.8 top right; p.9 top right; p.14; p.16–p.17;
p.33; p.35; p.36; p.39; p.41; p.43; p.47; p.54; p.61; p.65; p.69; p.73; p.77; p.81; p.91
Ken Scott: p.76; p.82
Mark Whitley (Flickr): p.9 top left
Pierre Gorissen (Flickr): p.62
Steve J O'Brien (Flickr): p.58
SuperStock, © Robert Harding Picture Library: p.18; p.51
Thinkstock: p.6 bottom; p.7 top, centre left, centre right, bottom left; p.8 top left, bottom left, bottom right;
p.9 bottom left, centre, bottom right; p.10; p.13; p.15; p.19; p.23; p.24; p.25; p.27; p.29; p.31; p.32; p.34; p.40;
p.44; p.45; p.48; p.50; p.52; p.55; p.56; p.57; p.59; p.64; p.66; p.67; p.71; p.72; p.74; p.75; p.78; p.80; p.83; p.84;
p.87; p.89; p.90

CONTENTS

INTRODUCTION

Castles were first built in Europe and the Middle East about a thousand years ago. The word 'castle' comes from the Latin word *castellum*, meaning 'fortress, fort, citadel, shelter or refuge'.

Castles were used primarily as residences, where the owners, usually royalty or the nobility, and their knights and attendants could live safely, retain their status and defend themselves against attackers.

 DID YOU KNOW?
The earliest surviving English document to use the word 'castle' is *The Anglo Saxon Chronicle* of 1051.

MULTIPLE FUNCTIONS

The idea of castles developed from the fortifications that had been used for centuries, designed for warfare defence (see p.10). But unlike the hill forts of the Iron Age, medieval castles combined several functions, serving equally as residences, fortresses and centres of administration. Intentionally imposing, they were almost invincible, built for defence and domination of the surrounding countryside.

NORMAN CASTLES

A few castles had been built before 1066 by Norman friends of Edward the Confessor (1003/5–66), but after the Battle of Hastings there was an explosion of castle building, as Norman lords took possession of land previously owned by the Anglo-Saxons. This was one of the main ways that the Normans sought to confirm their power and control of various regions across Britain.

More castles were built in England in the first century after the Norman invasion than at any other time. These unfamiliar and commanding buildings were built incredibly quickly using materials found nearby, such as wood, earth and fragments of rock. Seen for miles around, they announced the Norman lords' strength and authority and discouraged potential uprisings.

HIGH AND MIGHTY

At first the Normans built basic wooden motte and bailey structures (see p.18), but once they had established their control, they had time to build stronger and more permanent castles and from the late 1070s, the Normans built their castles in stone (see p.44).

The most protected part of every castle was the tower, originally referred to as the 'donjon' (meaning 'dominating point' in Latin), but later called the keep. Keeps were built in a variety of shapes and sizes and their form and function changed over time and varied depending on developments in weapon technology and a castle's location. For example, square keeps were replaced by more easily defended cylindrical or shell keeps in the 12th century.

In the late 13th century, during the reign of Edward I (1239–1307), the first concentric castles were built (see p.50).

Conwy Castle illuminated at night

Using only simple tools and local materials, there were often as many as 2,000 men working on one castle.

TIMES OF CHANGE

The great age of castle building was mainly between 1066 and 1485 in England and Wales and for about two centuries longer in Scotland.

Castles were built during times of insecurity and danger, when wars, feuds and rebellions were frequent occurrences. However, as new methods and tactics of warfare developed, castles were changed and their importance lessened. The aristocracy wanted more comfortable homes meaning that castles that were built in the 14th and 15th centuries often looked tough from the outside, but were normal domestic homes inside. They still remained difficult to heat and were often draughty, and so they began to lessen in popularity. Separate forts were built and manned solely by soldiers, while nobles built themselves grand residences using building material from old castles. Some castles became centres for local administration and some served as prisons, but never again did they achieve the importance they once had.

These were 'castles within castles'; complexes of buildings, towers and gatehouses, constructed within two or more defensive, curtain walls, which were even stronger against attack and siege than square or shell keeps. Although they had similarities such as battlements, towering heights, exceptionally thick walls and arrow slits, castles were not all alike and castle builders cleverly took advantage of unique natural features in each location.

WEIRD AND WONDERFUL

Nobody was allowed to build a castle unless they had received a 'Licence to Crenellate' from the king.

THE RISE AND FALL OF CASTLE BUILDING

During the most intense period of castle building, hundreds of massive, striking castles were constructed across Britain. Skilled workers were brought in from all parts of the kingdom, including master masons, quarrymen, woodcutters, smiths, miners, ditchers, carters and carpenters.

All over Britain, many of these castles still stand, some in ruins and some intact, many a mixture of various generations' building methods and styles. Rising above the landscape they appear romantic and remote, their rich histories of conflict, violence and power legendary and mysterious. They remain some of the most well-known and least understood buildings in Britain and some of the most enduring elements of its past.

TOP 10 HIGHLIGHTS

From Tintagel to Beaumaris and from Edinburgh to Conwy, these are just some of the breathtaking castles that characterise the British landscape.

1 **CAERNARFON CASTLE (P.60)**
On the banks of the River Seiont, the construction of mighty Caernarfon Castle was one of Edward I's powerful methods of controlling Wales.

2 **THE TOWER OF LONDON (P.16)**
The Tower of London began as a symbol of control by the Normans and has been used as a prison, a royal residence, a zoo and a storehouse.

3 **HEVER CASTLE (P.24)**
The childhood home of Anne Boleyn, Hever Castle is a charming Tudor residence with a massive gateway, double moat and walled bailey.

4 **BEAUMARIS CASTLE (P.64)**
The last and largest of the castles to be built by Edward I in Wales, Beaumaris is perfectly symmetrical, surrounded by a wide moat and considered by many to be the most perfect example of all his castles, even though it was never completed.

5 **EDINBURGH CASTLE (P.70)**
Strategically placed near the mouth of the River Forth, Edinburgh Castle, once a royal residence, still dominates the skyline of the city.

6 CONWY CASTLE (P.62)

A vast enclosure divided into an inner and outer ward with eight massive flanking towers, Conwy Castle was another of Edward I's symbols of power over the Welsh people.

7 WARWICK CASTLE (P.31)

Constructed on the site of a wooden fortress built to resist the Vikings, Warwick Castle has been the home to some influential figures such as Richard de Beauchamp, who supervised the trial of Joan of Arc, and Richard Neville who helped Edward IV to become king.

8 TINTAGEL CASTLE (P.27)

Half on the mainland and half on a peninsula, Tintagel Castle is remote and ruined from centuries of being exposed on the wild Cornish coast, but the atmosphere and mysteries of the legends of King Arthur make up for any missing walls.

9 STIRLING CASTLE (P.84)

One of the largest and most important castles in Scotland, Stirling Castle stands on the top of steep cliffs, the place of several Scottish coronations and eight sieges.

10 ALNWICK CASTLE (P.41)

The extraordinary mixture of styles found in Alnwick fit together like a fascinating jigsaw, revealing evidence of times of violence, unrest and elegant grandeur.

TIMELINE

12th century
Motte and bailey
Totnes Castle
See p.28

Iron Age
Early forts
Maiden Castle
See p.11

13th century
Concentric
Caernarfon Castle
See p.60

Iron Age	1000s	1100s	1200s	1300s

11th century
Norman
Dover Castle
See p.13

14th century
Medieval moated
Bodiam Castle
See p.25

15th century
Medieval
Tattershall Castle
See p.37

19th century
Scottish baronial
Balmoral Castle
See p.91

| 1400s | 1500s | 1600s | 1700s | 1800s |

17th century
L-plan tower house
Braemar Castle
See p.89

16th century
Tudor
St Mawes Castle
See p.29

18th century
Georgian country house
Floors Castle
See p.90

EARLY FORTS

Forts were forerunners to castles, first built in Britain during the Bronze and Iron Ages. They were large enclosures protected by ramparts and walls, built on high ground and surrounded by deep ditches.

BUILT FOR DEFENCE

Some forts were only used at certain times of the year or during periods of war, while others were occupied permanently. Built for defence, they were also symbols of power, meeting places, homes, refuges, trading centres and seats of administration and governance.

Forts varied in size, shape and design, but they also had similarities. All were built on hilltops or headlands and all were made of stone, soil and wood. Most had high fences, walls or palisades and some had parapets. Fort entrances were large wooden gates, with later forts having additional guardhouses on either side of the gates. Within the walls were wattle-and-daub thatched huts used for a variety of purposes and a defensive, look-out tower called a barbican.

The remains of Housesteads Roman Fort in Northumberland

These hill forts were built by the many Iron Age tribes. It is not known if they were built by native Britons to defend themselves from the intruding Celts or by the Celts as they settled in Britain.

WEIRD AND WONDERFUL

In battle, many Celtic warriors cut off the heads of enemies they had killed and displayed them at their temple entrances.

The Celts were warlike, but also extremely organised and sophisticated. The word 'Celt' comes from the Greek word *Keltoi* meaning 'barbarians' but this term was not used until the 18th century. Meanwhile the Picts, inhabitants of north-eastern Scotland, were building 'brochs' – big stone towers that they used as shelters in times of war.

DID YOU KNOW?

The Picts are often described as barbarians, but evidence shows that they were civilised people who produced advanced tools and defended themselves rather than attacked.

PRE-FABRICATED FORTS

Hundreds of workers were used for fort construction as a variety of skills were required, such as carpentry, blacksmithing, stone-cutting, transportation, digging

An example of a broch built by the Picts

and carrying. This huge workforce continued after the Roman conquest of Britain in AD43, when the invaders began building their own military fortifications and either abandoned or re-occupied many of the established Iron Age forts.

DID YOU KNOW?

Roman forts were made mostly of wood or stone, but some were constructed with the great Roman invention: concrete. Concrete was made by mixing volcanic ash, called *pozzolana*, with rubble and lime.

For nearly 400 years, the Romans continued building across Britain, filling their forts with soldiers to defend the surrounding land. As their fort designs always followed the same pattern, many were made with ready-made parts. They were always rectangular, large enough to accommodate up to 800 men with 9 metres high (30 ft) watchtowers and encircled by a wide ditch. Within the walls were essential buildings, including the commander's headquarters, dwellings, hospitals, workshops, barracks, granaries, stables and prisons.

WEIRD AND WONDERFUL

According to legend an ancient, mythical giant creature – the Lambton Worm – coiled round Penshaw Hill in northern England, creating the only triple rampart around an Iron Age fort.

MAIDEN CASTLE

Maiden Castle in Dorset is the largest and most complex Iron Age hill fort in Europe. Originally constructed in 600BC over the remains of a 6,000 year old Neolithic settlement, it is about 210 metres above sea level.

The Romans occupied and extended it until it took up an area the size of 50 football pitches and contained dwellings for several hundred people. Protected by rings of ditches and some 6 metre high ramparts, it was abandoned after the Romans left Britain. Its name evolved from its Iron Age description *Mai Dun*, which means 'Great Hill'.

IF YOU LIKED THIS...

Try visiting Maiden Castle near Dorchester or Danebury Hill Fort in Hampshire.

England: South East

Historically, the South East of England was vulnerable to attack from invaders. It was where William, Duke of Normandy landed and where he began his conquest of England, building castles as he went.

THE FORTRESS OF BRITAIN

No one was more aware than William the Conqueror of the need to protect this part of the country and as soon as he had won the Battle of Hastings, he set about building castles across the region. After his reign and until the late 14th century, monarchs built some of the most impressive and imposing castles in the area, strengthening its resistance and turning it into the fortress of Britain.

1. Dover	5. Windsor
2. Arundel	6. Carisbrooke
3. Lewes	7. Leeds
4. The Tower of London	8. Hever
	9. Bodiam

DOVER CASTLE

LOCATION: Harold's Road, Dover, Kent CT16 IHU
DATE BUILT: (original building) 1066
CASTLE STYLE: Late Norman
www.english-heritage.org.uk

Often called 'the gateway to England', Dover Castle stands on the site of the oldest fort in the country and has been used throughout its history, even playing a part in the two World Wars.

REINFORCING AUTHORITY

There was probably an Iron Age hill fort on the high cliffs above Dover when the Romans arrived and built a lighthouse on the site. Little is known about the following Anglo-Saxon fort, but within a month of the Battle of Hastings, William the Conqueror had taken possession of it and spent just eight days turning it into a motte and bailey castle (see p.18).

A castle has stood on Dover's cliffs for nearly 2,000 years

 DID YOU KNOW?
During the Napoleonic wars tunnels were built under the castle. During the Second World War the tunnels were used as a military command centre.

Over a century later, from 1168 to 1190, Henry II set about re-establishing his authority in England, giving Dover Castle three important new features: towered walls around the inner bailey, the beginning of a curtain wall and a massive square keep.

SECRET TUNNELS

In 1216, a group of rebel barons invited Louis VIII of France to take the English crown. The French army attacked Dover Castle, but were ultimately unable to take it. In response, Henry III strengthened the defences with a vast network of tunnels and new gates in the outer curtain wall.

In the second half of the 15th century, Edward IV modernised the keep and later, Henry VIII added some more fortifications. During the English Civil War, the castle was taken by Parliamentarians.

 IF YOU LIKED THIS...
You might also like Hedingham Castle, another towering Norman square keep.

England

ARUNDEL CASTLE

LOCATION: Arundel, West Sussex BN18 9AB
DATE BUILT: (original building) 1067
CASTLE STYLE: Norman
www.arundelcastle.org

Rising up from the trees above the River Arun near the south coast of England, Arundel Castle has an almost fairytale appearance, with its mix of Norman, medieval and 19th century neo-Gothic architecture.

BUILT IN STAGES

There has been a castle at Arundel since the first motte and bailey castle was built on the site of an earlier Saxon fortification nearly 1,000 years ago. In 1067, Roger de Montgomery, the newly created Earl of Arundel, had a castle constructed there. His motte was over 30 metres (100 feet) high and he added the gatehouse and part of the curtain wall in 1070. The rest of the curtain wall was built in stages during the 12th and 13th centuries.

On Montgomery's death, the castle passed to Henry I who left it to his widow, Adeliza of Louvain. Adeliza's second husband,

William d'Albini II, built the stone shell keep, but after he died Henry II restructured the building, adding walls, a chapel and a garden.

 DID YOU KNOW?
It is thought that Henry II's garden at Arundel was the first royal garden in England.

FAMILY CONTINUITY

Since 1138, Arundel Castle has passed almost directly through one family, only occasionally returning back to the Crown. Restoration was not undertaken until the 18th century, by the 11th Duke of Norfolk.

Established since Norman times, Arundel Castle remains a family home

LEWES CASTLE

LOCATION: High Street, Lewes, East Sussex BN7 1YE
DATE BUILT: 1069–70
CASTLE STYLE: Norman
www.sussexpast.co.uk

Situated high above the valley of the River Ouse near the South Downs, Lewes Castle was built in about 1069–70 by William de Warenne, the first Earl of Surrey and brother-in-law of William the Conqueror.

CHALK MOUNDS

With the unusual difference of having two mottes and one bailey (like Lincoln Castle; see p.32), Lewes Castle was constructed with defensive earthworks and a dry moat soon after the Norman invasion.

It stands at the highest point of Lewes, a little Saxon town 24 miles (39km) from Hastings, on two artificial mounds created with large chalk blocks. One motte is directly above the river and the second, more commanding motte is attached to the town wall.

THE BARBICAN

When Lewes Castle was built, the River Ouse was crossable and Lewes was a functional port on a significant river crossing. As William I's chief Justiciar (chief political and legal officer), Warenne made the castle his main residence.

The stone shell keep was built in the early 12th century and two semi-octagonal towers were added in the following century, with the barbican built approximately 100 years after that.

Made of flint rubble with a machicolated parapet (a barrier with holes in it, for dropping missiles on attackers), the barbican overlooks the site of the Battle of Lewes, which was fought in 1264, when Simon de Montfort and the barons defeated Henry III and occupied the town.

WEIRD AND WONDERFUL

In 1382, the citizens of Lewes rioted and plundered the castle, selling off much of the stone as building material.

Lewes Castle has one of the best preserved barbicans in England

THE TOWER OF LONDON

LOCATION: Tower Hill, London EC3N 4AB
DATE BUILT: c.1078–98
CASTLE STYLE: Norman
www.hrp.org.uk/TowerOfLondon

When the defeated English army returned to London in 1066, William the Conqueror followed. He immediately ordered the construction of a castle on the north bank of the River Thames within the Roman city walls.

TORTURE AND EXECUTION

An ultimate symbol of power, the Tower of London is probably the most famous castle in the world. Although it has functioned as a storehouse for weapons, public records and the crown jewels, a zoo and a shelter for some monarchs and dignitaries, it was mainly a formidable fortress. Some of the most powerful people in the land were imprisoned, tortured and executed within its walls. Many prisoners were brought by barge

along the River Thames and entered through Traitors' Gate.

WEIRD AND WONDERFUL

Of the 63 bodies in the Chapel Royal of St Peter ad Vincula within the Tower of London, only 10 were buried with their heads still on.

ENHANCED DEFENCES

Construction of the stone tower keep started in 1078 and was completed in 1097. Practically square in design, it dominated the land from all angles. Built of a mixture of stone from Kent and France, the castle was protected by Roman walls on two sides.

Both Henry III and Edward I made huge and expensive improvements. Henry III enhanced the defences and Edward I completed the outer curtain wall and set up the Royal Mint there. By the mid-14th century, the Tower had taken on its basic concentric plan. Since then minor additions and improvements have been made within the inner bailey, such as the Queen's House during the reign of Henry VIII.

IF YOU LIKED THIS...

Explore more of the Tower, with its sights and stories of significant events in the history of the British monarchy, including Henry VIII's armour, the site of several executions and the crown jewels.

The Tower of London was built by William I to intimidate the people of London

MOTTE AND BAILEY CASTLES

As soon as William I won the Battle of Hastings in 1066 he set about confirming his command of the country. His men spread rapidly across England, building wooden motte and bailey castles.

An aerial view of Carisbrooke Castle

WOOD TO STONE

William actually built his first castle in England before the Battle of Hastings. As soon as he landed on English soil, two weeks before the battle, he raised a castle on the site of an old Roman fort in Pevensey, just under 12 miles (19km) from Hastings, to house his men and to display his power to the local inhabitants. After his success in battle, he continued building castles as symbols of his might and power.

Central to the feudal system (see p.66), these early castles were mainly motte and baileys made of wood and earth. These castles were built on a raised earthwork mound (motte) and surrounded by a protective fence (bailey). Whenever there was enough time, money and manpower,

stronger and more secure stone castles were built instead.

 DID YOU KNOW?
As soon as William was crowned, he began his campaign to subdue the Saxons, seizing their estates to give them to his followers.

VISIBLE WARNINGS

Although William knew that his wooden castles were not permanent – the wood rotted quickly and they could easily be destroyed by fire – they had immediate value as visible warnings, there to crush any rebels. Because motte and bailey castles were made mainly in timber, often making use of the natural landscape, they did not require a skilled labour force to build them, so they could be built quickly – some within a couple of weeks.

 DID YOU KNOW?
In the 12th century, when a skilled labourer earned just two pence a day, Rochester Castle cost approximately £3,000 to build and Dover Castle cost about £4,000.

ESSENTIAL FEATURES

These early Norman castles were constructed in many shapes and sizes, depending on requirements and resources. While there was no single design, there were certain essential requirements. They had to be built on the highest points, often near to rivers, towns or harbours and they were often built on the existing foundations of Roman or Saxon forts.

The motte or huge mound of earth, distinguished them from the earlier Anglo-Saxon defences and with their wooden towers rising from the motte, they were both eye-catching and intimidating. Encircled by a timber fence, the area around the motte was known as a bailey, which ranged from between two and 10 acres and was used for stabling and grazing, growing crops, and contained servants' quarters, workshops and a chapel.

If a castle was attacked, success in defending it depended on how organised the inhabitants were, but especially on how well the castle had been built. Mainly used for defence and offence, the castles were also where the Norman lords and their families lived, entertained guests and used as places of refuge, so they needed to be fairly comfortable and to show that the lord had wealth, power and status.

LIFE IN A FEUDAL SOCIETY

Life in motte and bailey castles was quite self-contained. The lord of the castle and his family lived in the keep – the most protected part of the castle. As part of the feudal system enforced by the Normans, the king granted land to a lord in return for the lord's support and the land was worked by freemen and serfs or villeins, who in return, were protected by the lord.

The feudal economy was based on land and services rather than money – but the Norman lords who had supported William I profited hugely.

 WEIRD AND WONDERFUL
From c.1070 until around 1200, it is thought that nearly 1,000 motte and bailey castles were built by the Normans.

A motte (raised mound of earth) like those built by William I

England

WINDSOR CASTLE

LOCATION: St Leonard's Road, Windsor, Berkshire SL4 3BX
DATE BUILT: c.1080
CASTLE STYLE: Norman
www.royalcollection.org.uk

The largest and oldest inhabited castle in the world, Windsor Castle has been renovated and enlarged by various rulers since it was built by William the Conqueror.

MAIN DEVELOPMENTS

Originally constructed as a motte and bailey castle in c.1080 close to a royal hunting forest, Windsor Castle was unusual in having a central motte and two baileys. Successive monarchs have expanded and reinforced the castle, which stands an impressive 30 metres (100 feet) above the River Thames.

DID YOU KNOW?
Windsor is the only royal castle that has been in almost continuous occupation since the Middle Ages.

In the 1170s, Henry II remodelled the great Round Tower, as well as some of the outer walls and the royal apartments. Two centuries later, Edward III, who was born at Windsor, began its main transformations. In addition to a suite of royal apartments, he created the vast St George's Hall for his knights and newly founded Order of the Garter. In 1477, Edward IV began building St George's Chapel, which was continued by Henry VII and completed by Henry VIII in 1528.

WARFARE

In the early 13th century, the castle withstood a lengthy siege during the First Barons' War. At the beginning of the English Civil War in 1642, Oliver Cromwell captured the castle and turned it into a prison as well as his Parliamentary forces' headquarters. Charles I was held there in 1648 before his trial and execution in London and his body was brought back for burial in St George's Chapel.

DID YOU KNOW?
At the end of the Civil War in 1649, a Parliamentary bill to demolish Windsor Castle was stopped by just one vote.

GOTHIC REVIVAL

Following the restoration of the monarchy in the 1670s, Charles II created some new state apartments. Few changes were made after that until George IV employed the architect Sir Jeffrey Wyatville in the 1820s to 'modernise' the castle in the Gothic style, with the addition of crenellations, gargoyles, turrets and towers.

An aerial view of Windsor Castle showing its grand scale

WEIRD AND WONDERFUL

Charles II had a new plumbing system installed in the castle. The inventor, Samuel Morland, demonstrated that it was working by creating a huge fountain filled with wine.

Queen Victoria used Windsor as her main residence, but made few changes. During the Second World War, the young Princesses Elizabeth and Margaret lived there. After a serious fire in 1992, 100 damaged rooms were restored, either to their original designs or in a modern Gothic style. Today, Queen Elizabeth II spends many weekends at the castle.

ROYAL BURIALS

Ten British monarchs are buried in the chapel: Edward IV, Henry VI, Henry VIII, Charles I, George III, George IV, William IV, Edward VII, George V and George VI. Prince Albert died of typhoid at Windsor in 1861 and was buried in a spectacular mausoleum that Queen Victoria constructed at Frogmore in the Windsor Home Park.

DID YOU KNOW?

Henry VIII is buried at Windsor with his third wife, Jane Seymour, the mother of their son. She is the only one of his six wives buried with him.

IF YOU LIKED THIS...

The architecture of Windsor has many similarities with Kenilworth Castle in Warwickshire and Warkworth Castle in Northumberland.

England

CARISBROOKE CASTLE

LOCATION: Castle Hill, Isle of Wight PO30 1XY
DATE BUILT: 1070
CASTLE STYLE: Norman motte and bailey
www.english-heritage.org.uk

Built on the site of an Anglo-Saxon fort, Carisbrooke began as a simple motte and bailey castle, but was extended to become an elaborate fortress and served as Charles I's prison.

EXPANSION

There was a fort on the site of Carisbrooke Castle in late Roman times and another during the eighth century. By 1000, a wall was constructed as defence against Viking raids. In 1070, when William FitzOsbern, Earl of Hereford, was given command of the Isle of Wight, he built a castle on the site (see also Chepstow Castle, p.47).

In 1100, in the first year of his reign, Henry I granted the castle to Richard de Redvers. For the next 200 years, the Redvers family turned it into a mighty castle with thick walls, towers and a great shell keep. Edward I then bought the castle in 1292.

ATTACK AND DETAIN

Carisbrooke fought off a French siege in 1377. In 1588, the Spanish Armada came disturbingly near, so the castle was refortified once more with artillery defences, but it was used more frequently as a prison than in defence. The most famous prisoner was Charles I, who detained there from November 1647 to September 1648, just five months before his execution at Whitehall.

A view through the gatehouse of Carisbrooke Castle

There are two wells within the castle. One is reached by 71 steps and the other was originally worked by Carisbrooke's prisoners, until donkeys were used from the 17th century.

DID YOU KNOW?
Charles I tried to escape Carisbrooke Castle twice but was caught both times. In one attempt, he became wedged in the window bars of his room.

LEEDS CASTLE

 LOCATION: Maidstone, Kent ME17 1PL
DATE BUILT: 1119
CASTLE STYLE: Late Norman
www.leeds-castle.com

Shrouded in mystery, Leeds Castle rises from a lake in over 500 acres of lush parkland. First constructed during the late Norman period, it became a royal residence for several kings and six medieval queens.

ROYAL PALACE

In the mid-ninth century, a manor house called Esledes, owned by a Saxon royal family, was situated on the current site of Leeds Castle, on two small islands in a lake formed by the River Len. The name *esledes* is an old English word meaning 'slope' or 'hillside' and it is from this that the name Leeds evolved. In 1119, Robert de Crèvecœur built a stone castle on the site. In 1278 Leeds Castle was given to Edward I and his queen, Eleanor of Castile, and it remained in royal possession for 300 years. Edward I made several additions, including a chapel when his beloved wife died in 1290.

THE LADIES' CASTLE

Often called the ladies' castle, Leeds has been gifted to more queens than most, including Richard II's wife, Anne of Bohemia, Edward III's wife, Margaret of France and Henry V's wife, Catherine de Valois. When Henry VIII married Catherine of Aragon in 1512, he made some extravagant improvements. Conversely, Elizabeth I was imprisoned there for a while before her coronation.

 WEIRD AND WONDERFUL

Eleanor Cobham, Duchess of Gloucester, was accused of trying to assassinate her husband's nephew, Henry VI, using witchcraft. She was confined in Leeds Castle until her trial.

Leeds Castle stands on islands surrounded by a river and extensive grounds

England

HEVER CASTLE

LOCATION: Near Edenbridge, Kent TN8 7NG
DATE BUILT: c.1270
CASTLE STYLE: Medieval moated castle
www.hevercastle.co.uk

This charming castle is famous for its connections with Anne Boleyn. Originating in the 13th century, it began as a moated manor house, built on land granted to a Norman lord by William the Conqueror.

HOUSE TO CASTLE

In about 1270, during the reign of Henry III, William de Hevere built a stone moated manor house on the land granted to his ancestor soon after the Norman Conquest. For greatest impact, he added a massive gatehouse, walled bailey and a wooden drawbridge. After passing through several hands, a licence to crenellate the property (build a castle) was granted in about 1340.

ANNE BOLEYN

In 1459 Sir Geoffrey Bullen, a wealthy merchant who had been Lord Mayor of

London, bought the castle. He converted and extended the building and by 1505, his son Sir Thomas (who changed his name to Boleyn at the end of the 15th century) inherited it and made further improvements.

Sir Thomas lived at Hever with his wife Elizabeth, daughter of the Duke of Norfolk and their three children, George, Anne and Mary. Anne grew up at Hever and was courted by Henry VIII there before she became his second wife in 1533. After Anne's execution and her father's death, Hever became the property of the Crown and in 1540 Henry VIII gave it to his fourth wife, Anne of Cleves, as part of her divorce settlement. She owned Hever until her death in 1557.

WEIRD AND WONDERFUL

When Anne Boleyn was beheaded in 1536 no coffin had been prepared, so her body and severed head were put in an elm-wood arrow chest.

Hever Castle was the childhood home of Anne Boleyn

BODIAM CASTLE

LOCATION: Robertsbridge, East Sussex TN32 5UA
DATE BUILT: 1385–88
CASTLE STYLE: Medieval moated castle
www.nationaltrust.org.uk

In 1385, Sir Edward Dalyngrigge was granted a licence by Richard II to fortify his manor house, as protection for his family and to defend the surrounding countryside against the threat of invasion from France.

DEFENCE AND COMFORT

In the 14th and 15th centuries, castles were more often built by wealthy members of the public than by kings or dukes. Master craftsmen from all over Europe created Bodiam, incorporating some of the most advanced features of castle design.

Surrounded by a deep and wide moat fed by natural springs, it emerges from the water, perfectly symmetrical, with round towers at each corner and square towers midway along each wall. The walls, made of massive stone blocks, are on average 2 metres thick, although this is not particularly thick for a castle. There are also three drawbridges, a system of bridges, a gatehouse and three portcullises.

Although the castle reflected warfare developments of the time, with gun ports built into the gatehouse alongside the arrow slits, more importance was given to comfort than to defence. The castle was designed to withstand quick raids rather than prolonged attacks and was completed within about five years.

Bodiam Castle appears both romantic and menacing

 DID YOU KNOW?
Although castle building continued in Scotland until the 17th century, Bodiam was one of the last medieval castles to be built in England.

COMFORTABLE LIVING

Those living at Bodiam were extremely self-sufficient. A spring-fed well provided water; fruit and vegetables were grown in the gardens; bees were kept for honey; livestock for meat and poultry for eggs. Grain from the surrounding fields was also stored inside the castle.

England: South West

Although heavily populated by various settlers throughout its early history, and surrounded and dominated by the sea, the South West of England did not really integrate with the country it was attached to.

ASSIMILATION

The South West was the last part of Roman Britain to hold out against Saxon invaders. It was only after the Norman Conquest that the people began to assimilate with the rest of England. In 1068, William the Conqueror and his forces marched in a vast circuit around England, travelling to the South West directly after the South East, building castles as they went.

1. Tintagel

2. Totnes

3. St Mawes

TINTAGEL CASTLE

LOCATION: Bossiney Road, Tintagel, Cornwall PL34 0HE
DATE BUILT: (current visible remains) c.1227–33
CASTLE STYLE: Late medieval
www.english-heritage.org.uk

Standing high on the rugged Cornish coast, Tintagel Castle is steeped in myth and mystery. Traditionally associated with the legendary King Arthur, the castle's history is believed to stretch back to Roman times.

EARLY OCCUPATION

Clinging to a rocky headland against the wild north Cornish coast, Tintagel has been beaten by the Atlantic Ocean for centuries. Over time, much of the slate rock it was built with has been swept away by the sea. The remaining ruins are of a castle built by Richard, Earl of Cornwall (1209–72), King John's second son in c.1227–33, but the site might have been originally occupied by the Romans.

KING ARTHUR

Whether or not Tintagel did experience a period as a Roman military settlement, during the fifth and sixth centuries it became a dwelling place for Celtic kings of Cornwall and one of those is thought to have been King Arthur. The castle of that period is said to be the legendary Camelot where Arthur held his famous court with the round table – although several other British castles make the same claim! In the middle of the 12th century, Geoffrey of Monmouth (c.1100–55) wrote his *History of the Kings of Britain*, which first told the story of King Arthur and linked his name with Tintagel.

The remains of Tintagel on the windswept headland

DID YOU KNOW?

Other legends about Tintagel include the story of the medieval King Mark, who caused the death of the Cornish knight Tristan and his love, the beautiful princess Isolde.

SURROUNDED BY THE SEA

Tintagel stands high on a cliff in western Cornwall, surrounded on three sides by the Atlantic Ocean. Derelict since the 16th century, the desolate and remote spot remains awe-inspiring and atmospheric.

TOTNES CASTLE

LOCATION: Castle Street, Totnes, Devon TQ9 5NU
DATE BUILT: 1100
CASTLE STYLE: Norman
www.english-heritage.org.uk

Shortly after the Norman Conquest, Judhael de Totnes, one of William the Conqueror's knights, built a motte and bailey castle above the River Dart to watch over the inhabitants of the Saxon town below.

THREE VALLEYS

Judhael had been one of William's lieutenants on a campaign to crush a rebellion in the South West of England. As soon as William granted him the land Judhael built the castle to assert his control. Using layers of earth, rock and clay on natural rock, he constructed a huge mound above the town at a point where three valleys meet.

NO CONFLICT

Judhael lost his lands on William I's death and in 1219 the original square wooden tower was replaced with a stone shell keep and curtain walls by Reginald de Braose. The castle was completed by the early 14th century and it remains one of the largest mottes and best preserved shell keeps in the country, which probably never faced any conflict.

By 1326, the castle had fallen into ruin and the owners at the time, the de la Zouch family, received a royal order to refortify it. They appointed a constable who maintained the keep but left the buildings in the bailey to deteriorate even more.

From 1485, after the Wars of the Roses, the castle was neglected. It was briefly reoccupied during the Civil War, but was not involved in any fighting.

 IF YOU LIKED THIS...
Try visiting Launceston Castle in Cornwall or Okehampton Castle in Devon.

Totnes Castle was originally built to dominate the town

ST MAWES CASTLE

LOCATION: Castle Drive, Near Truro, Cornwall TR2 5DE
DATE BUILT: 1540–45
CASTLE STYLE: Tudor
www.english-heritage.org.uk

Taking decisive action against possible invasion from Catholic France and Spain, Henry VIII built several fortifications along the south coast of England, including St Mawes Castle in Cornwall.

DEVICE FORTS

When Henry VIII created his role of Defender of the Faith in England, cutting himself and his country off from Rome, the Pope began threatening a crusade against him. In response Henry built a series of forts to protect the south coast from potential invasion.

St Mawes Castle took approximately five years to complete, from 1540 to 1545, and cost £5,000 to build. Pendennis Castle was built on the opposite headland at the same time so that between the two castles, their cannons could cover the Fal Estuary. These coastal fortifications became known as Henrician castles or device forts, but unlike most castles, they were never intended to be residences as well as fortifications.

VULNERABILITY

St Mawes Castle has a central circular four-floored tower with three lower semi-circular bastions. The roof was designed as a gun platform and the small domed turret was intended as a look-out point. However, the castle was never attacked by the French or the

St Mawes is a low building with massively thick walls

Spanish and during Elizabeth I's reign, only Pendennis was enlarged. During the English Civil War, St Mawes Castle was a Royalist stronghold and, realising its vulnerability from a land attack, the governor surrendered without a shot being fired.

 DID YOU KNOW?
St Mawes is one of the most decorated of Henry VIII's castle forts. Elaborate gargoyles, detailed windows and carved inscriptions throughout contrast with his plainer fortifications.

England: Central

With some of the most important English cities of the Middle Ages, like the rest of the country, central England witnessed an immense castle-building programme shortly after the Battle of Hastings.

MOMENTOUS EVENTS

Many of the castles built by the Normans across the middle of England were constructed on the sites of earlier fortifications, such as Warwick and Colchester Castles. Others are the locations of momentous historical events, such as Berkeley Castle where the alleged murder of Edward II is said to have taken place, and Framlingham Castle where Mary I gathered her forces before marching on London as Queen of England.

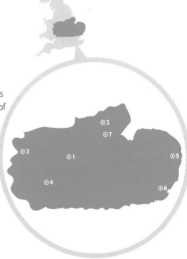

1. Warwick

2. Lincoln

3. Ludlow

4. Goodrich

5. Framlingham

6. Orford

7. Tattershall

WARWICK CASTLE

 LOCATION: Warwick, Warwickshire CV34 4QU
DATE BUILT: (original building) 1068
CASTLE STYLE: Norman
www.warwick-castle.com

William the Conqueror built Warwick Castle in timber and earth in 1068. Twenty years later, it passed to the first Earl of Warwick and over the next three centuries it was substantially rebuilt.

SIGNIFICANT OWNERS

Warwick Castle began as an earthen fortification built in AD914 to resist the Danes and in 1088 it became the seat of the influential Earls of Warwick. 154 years later a Norman motte and bailey castle was built on the site and it was rebuilt again in the mid-13th century with a stone shell keep and curtain walls.

KINGMAKER

Richard Neville (1428–71), the 16th Earl of Warwick, was the wealthiest, most powerful and popular English noble of his era, so influential in the removal of two kings and in securing the throne for Edward IV, that he became known as 'Kingmaker'. For the first few years of Edward IV's reign, Neville practically ruled England.

 DID YOU KNOW?
The name Warwick means 'dwellings by the weir'; a weir was a fence built across a stream to catch fish.

LAVISH RENOVATIONS

In 1264 during the Barons' Revolt, the shell keep was largely destroyed and most

Looking up at the clock tower of Warwick Castle

of the castle's present outer features date from the mid-14th century when it had passed to the Beauchamp family. A gatehouse and barbican were added, as were two large towers known as Guy's Tower and Caesar's Tower. The castle's defences were strengthened in the 1640s, helping it withstand a siege by Royalist forces in the English Civil War. The castle and grounds were luxuriously refurbished in the 18th century.

England

LINCOLN CASTLE

LOCATION: Castle Hill, Lincoln LN1 3AA
DATE BUILT: (original building) 1068
CASTLE STYLE: Norman
www.lincolnshire.gov.uk

In 1068, William the Conqueror had 166 Saxon houses demolished in Lincoln to make room for a castle. Built on the site of a Roman fort, William's structure was a simple motte and bailey castle.

STRATEGIC PRESENCE

By Norman times, Lincoln was an important trading town, so in addition to being a good spot from which to control English rebels, it was a strategic place for the Normans to have a presence.

They built Lincoln Castle quickly with wood and earth, although it was later replaced with a stronger stone structure. Part of the Roman wall was retained and the immense 12th century curtain wall remains.

 DID YOU KNOW?
In Viking times, Lincoln was a successful trading centre that issued coins from its own mint.

TWO MOTTES

Unusually, Lincoln Castle has two mottes and one bailey (Lewes Castle is the only other example of this, see p.15). In 1136, the owner of the castle, Lucy, Countess of Chester died, passing it to her son Ranulf. He built a strong shell keep which became known as the Lucy Tower. The second, smaller motte features a square tower with a 19th century observatory.

The Lucy Tower is one of the main surviving parts of Lincoln Castle

During a siege in the Barons' War in the 13th century, a new barbican was built onto the west and east gates, but the castle was damaged several times and the Civil War essentially ended its use as a stronghold.

Between 1787 and 1878, it was the city's prison and for 900 years the castle has been a centre of justice.

LUDLOW CASTLE

 LOCATION: Castle Square, Ludlow, Shropshire SY8 1AY
DATE BUILT: c.1085
CASTLE STYLE: Norman motte and bailey
www.ludlowcastle.com

'The very perfection of decay' is how Daniel Defoe described Ludlow Castle in 1722. The castle had originally been built in the late 11th century to guard the lawless Welsh Marcher Lords.

A LINE OF CASTLES

Built in about 1085 by Roger de Lacy whose father Walter was one of William FitzOsbern's retainers, Ludlow Castle was one of a line of castles constructed near the borders of England and Wales.

For two centuries, the de Lacy family held the castle, except for a time during the conflict for the English throne between Stephen and Matilda. In 1138, the castle was held by one of Matilda's supporters and the following year, Stephen (unsuccessfully) besieged it.

Ludlow Castle is a mix of early Norman buildings and 16th century expansion

 ## WEIRD AND WONDERFUL

In 1139, Ludlow was under siege by Stephen, when he saw his ally, Prince Henry of Scotland, being hung on a metal hook from the castle. Quickly, the king cut the rope and freed the prince.

LAVISH EXTENSIONS

At the beginning of the 14th century, Ludlow Castle came into the possession of Roger Mortimer, the Queen's lover and leader of a group of barons who overthrew Edward II. Mortimer extended the castle, but in 1330 he was executed for his involvement in Edward II's murder.

By the early 15th century, the castle was a base for Yorkists when it was attacked and robbed by Lancastrians. In 1461, Edward IV took the throne and Ludlow became Crown property. Edward IV's son grew up there and Wales and the border counties were managed from the castle.

It was besieged by Parliamentarians in the Civil War and finally abandoned in 1669 when government control moved to a central base in London.

33

 England

GOODRICH CASTLE

LOCATION: Castle Lane, Goodrich, Herefordshire HR9 6HY
DATE BUILT: c.1080s
CASTLE STYLE: Originally timber motte and bailey
www.english-heritage.org.uk

Goodrich Castle was built, like so many, as a timber and earth motte and bailey, but it was reconstructed between 1280 and 1320 to imitate many features of the castles over the border in Wales.

ORIGINAL BUILDING

The initial building of Goodrich Castle was begun by Godric Mappestone, probably in about 1087 in wood and earth. Sometime between 1138 and 1153, a sturdy sandstone keep was raised by Richard de Clare, Earl of Pembroke and Lord of Goodrich.

In 1204, Goodrich was granted to William Marshal, Earl of Pembroke (who also rebuilt Chepstow, p.47 and Pembroke Castles, p.49). Marshal added further buildings to Goodrich and after the last of his sons died in 1245, the castle passed to William de Valence, the husband of Marshal's niece and half-brother of Henry III.

William de Valence and his son Aymer spent the next 50 years rebuilding the castle, combining strong defences with luxurious living quarters, using light grey stone that contrasts with the earlier red sandstone.

The success of the castle's later concentric design influenced many other English castle builders for years.

PARLIAMENTARY SIEGE

In the early 14th century, Goodrich became the seat of the powerful Talbot family, but it was unoccupied in the early part of the Civil War until a Parliamentary force moved in, soon expelled by Royalists and finally attacked by Parliamentarians who reduced it to a ruin.

 IF YOU LIKED THIS...
Visit Harlech Castle (see p.61) over the border in Wales as the two castles have many elements in common.

Great walls are leftovers of Goodrich's formidable past

FRAMLINGHAM CASTLE

LOCATION: Woodbridge, Suffolk IP13 9BP
DATE BUILT: 1177
CASTLE STYLE: Norman
www.english-heritage.org.uk

A motte and bailey castle was built on the Framlingham site by 1148, but Henry II ordered its destruction in 1174. The castle that survives today was built after that by the second Earl of Norfolk.

OPPOSING THE KING

Henry II ordered Framlingham to be destroyed after the 1st Earl of Norfolk, Hugh Bigod, had joined the king's sons in the attempt to overthrow him. Nevertheless, not much of the castle was damaged and Hugh's son Roger began rebuilding it in 1177.

Taking almost 40 years to complete, the castle had no central keep and 13 towers breaking the curtain wall at regular intervals.

RAISING THE ROYAL STANDARD

Continuing the family history of defying its kings, in 1216 Roger Bigod entered into conflict with King John. Although the king took the castle after a short siege he died shortly afterwards, allowing the Bigod family to retake it.

In 1553, Edward VI gave Framlingham to his half-sister Mary, who was living there when he died and she became Queen of England. She raised her standard and gathered her forces at Framlingham before successfully marching on London to claim her throne.

Framlingham Castle at sunset

In the early 17th century, the castle fell into decay and in 1663 Framlingham was left to Pembroke College, Cambridge. The Great Hall and other internal buildings were demolished to make room for a poorhouse.

WEIRD AND WONDERFUL

In 1385–86, about 83 people lived in Framlingham and over £1,000 (about £450,000 now) was spent on provisions, including 28,567 gallons (129,868 litres) of ale and 70,321 loaves of bread.

England

ORFORD CASTLE

LOCATION: Woodbridge, Suffolk, IP12 2ND
DATE BUILT: 1166
CASTLE STYLE: Norman
www.english-heritage.org.uk

Built by Henry II so he could monitor the troublesome barons of East Anglia, Orford Castle is a remarkable 21-sided tower with three projecting square turrets.

COMPLEX STRUCTURE

When Henry II built Orford Castle – in just six years from 1166 to 1172 – it cost about £1,500. Records do not relate how it was built in its complex structure, but the design is believed to be based on Byzantine architecture. Some of the materials for the building were brought from Scarborough, Northamptonshire and from Caen in Normandy.

The tower was once surrounded by a curtain wall with rectangular towers placed at intervals along it and a twin-towered gatehouse.

DAUNTING DESIGN

The castle's purpose was to protect the shoreline from foreign invasion, but more pressingly, to assert Henry II's authority over local lords. He was just in time. In 1173, his three sons began a rebellion against him, and the Earl of Norfolk, Hugh Bigod (see p.35), helped other lords to land on the Suffolk coast to attack the king's castles. They took Haughley and Norwich, but did not attack Orford. The design of the keep may have discouraged them and the castle had a relatively uneventful history.

The unique polygonal keep of Orford Castle

It was captured only once in 1216 by Prince Louis of France who had been invited to invade England by the English barons who were disappointed with King John.

IF YOU LIKED THIS...
Try visiting Conisbrough Castle in South Yorkshire with its high circular keep and six wedge-shaped buttresses, built by Henry II's illegitimate half-brother Hamelin Plantagenet.

TATTERSHALL CASTLE

 LOCATION: Sleaford Road, Tattershall, Lincolnshire LN4 4LR
DATE BUILT: 1434
CASTLE STYLE: Red brick medieval
www.nationaltrust.org.uk

A fortified manor house was first built in stone on this site in 1231 by Robert de Tateshale, but all that remains of Tattershall Castle today is the red brick keep built two centuries later.

LOCAL BRICKS

Ralph, the third Baron Cromwell, inherited Tattershall Castle in the 15th century when he became Lord Treasurer to Henry VI from 1433 to 1443. Between 1434 and 1446, he built his great red brick tower over the demolished remains of the original stone building. Stone was readily available for the new castle, but Cromwell chose to use red brick because it was fashionable and impressive. Bricks had become popular in Britain during the 14th century when Flemish refugees took them into East Anglia.

Built more for fashion than defence Tattershall's red brick stands out

About a million bricks, made on site, were used to create the medieval brick residence.

EMBELLISHMENTS

Despite the thickness of the walls of Tattershall, the defensive elements were really decorative. With three separate doors on the ground floor and large windows, the castle was clearly built more for comfort than for defence.

The towering keep contains six floors, including a vaulted basement and battlements. The state rooms were once magnificent, with huge fireplaces and colourful tapestries and wall hangings. Several bridges and small gatehouses once stood around the two moats of the castle, adding to the impression of a great fortification.

 DID YOU KNOW?
The cost of building Tattershall's keep was over £3,000 (over £1 million today) and Lord Cromwell's household consisted of 100 people, which cost him about £5,000 a year (over £2 million).

England: North

Notoriously dangerous, for centuries the northernmost regions of England were susceptible to attack from Scotland. During Roman times, a line of forts was built to defend the English-Scottish borders.

ATTACKS ON THE NORTH

With a rich history, the northern counties of England were cultured and important until the Norman invasion when the area was desolated by the 'Harrying of the North'. This was a series of campaigns led by William the Conqueror in the winter of 1069–70 to conquer northern England and break its independence and power. After that, a huge building programme was undertaken with a great deal of castle-building.

1. Skipton

2. Carlisle

3. Alnwick

4. Warkworth

5. Conisbrough

SKIPTON CASTLE

 LOCATION: The Bailey, Skipton, North Yorkshire BD23 1AW
DATE BUILT: c.1090
CASTLE STYLE: Norman
www.skiptoncastle.co.uk

Although it dates from Norman times, Skipton is strongly associated with the English Civil War when it was nearly destroyed. It was later restored and is now one of the best preserved medieval castles in England.

RESISTING THE SCOTS

Built in 1090 by Robert de Romille, a Norman baron, Skipton Castle was originally a timber motte and bailey. The defences were later rebuilt in stone to resist attacks from the Scots.

In 1307 Edward II gave the castle to Piers Gaveston but three years later Gaveston was murdered by the king's enemies. Subsequently, in 1310, the king granted the castle to Robert de Clifford, appointing him Lord Clifford of Skipton.

Clifford immediately began to strengthen the fortifications but he was killed at the Battle of Bannockburn in 1314, leaving the work to be continued by his son. Between fighting for successive kings, the Clifford family made many improvements to the castle, including several circular towers in the gatehouse and bailey.

THREE YEAR SIEGE

Through the generations, the Clifford family remained loyal to the Crown and as a Royalist stronghold during the Civil War Skipton withstood a three-year siege by Parliamentary forces, surrendering eventually with honour in 1645.

Skipton was the last northern castle to resist Oliver Cromwell

The castle was partially demolished to prevent any further military use and although it was restored in the 1650s, it was forbidden to be returned to its former strength.

 ## WEIRD AND WONDERFUL

Legend says that during the Civil War, sheep fleeces were hung on Skipton Castle walls to reduce the impact of cannon fire. Accordingly, sheep fleeces feature on the town's coat of arms.

39

CARLISLE CASTLE

 LOCATION: Bridge Street, Carlisle, Cumbria CA3 8UR
DATE BUILT: c.1092
CASTLE STYLE: Norman
www.english-heritage.org.uk

Guarding the western end of the border between England and Scotland, Carlisle Castle was first built in c.1092 by William II. The wooden palisaded enclosure was built on the site of an earlier Roman fort.

CONFLICT AND CHANGE

The first motte and bailey castle was a simple wooden structure and in 1122, Henry I rebuilt it in stone. The keep and castle walls were completed by the Scottish king, David I, who took control of northern England during the problematic reign of Stephen (1135–54), but Henry II of England retook the castle in 1157.

When Edward I invaded Scotland, he used the castle as his headquarters and seat of government and so modernised it. Later, Richard II carried out more construction and repair on the castle from 1378 to 1383.

In 1461, during the Wars of the Roses, Carlisle came under siege by the Lancastrians and in 1541, the threat of a Franco-Scottish invasion drove Henry VIII to make further refurbishments.

SIEGE AND SEIZURE

In 1568, Mary, Queen of Scots was held prisoner at Carlisle and during the English Civil War, the castle was subjected to an eight-month siege by Parliamentarian forces. The last time it was besieged was in 1745. Prince Charles Edward Stuart's Jacobite forces captured the castle, but were forced to surrender a month later. The castle continued to be used as a barracks late into the 20th century.

 WEIRD AND WONDERFUL

There are 'licking stones' in the dungeon of Carlisle Castle where Jacobite prisoners licked moisture off the walls to keep themselves alive.

The medieval fortress defended the border

ALNWICK CASTLE

 LOCATION: Alnwick, Northumberland NE66 1NQ
DATE BUILT: 1096
CASTLE STYLE: Norman
www.alnwickcastle.com

Built in 1096 by Yves de Vescy, Baron of Alnwick, this is the second-largest occupied castle in the country. Over time, it has survived many conflicts and has been vastly extended by successive generations.

ORDER FOR DESTRUCTION

Alnwick Castle's position near the border with Scotland made it vulnerable to attack, so within 50 years, Yves de Vescy's timber motte and bailey castle was reconstructed in stone. The castle was the site of many clashes, including sieges in 1172 and 1174, by the Scottish king, William the Lion. In 1212, after Eustace de Vescy had helped to lead the Barons' Revolt, King John ordered the destruction of Alnwick Castle, but his orders were never carried out.

In 1309 Henry Percy bought the castle and the Barony of Alnwick. Henry and his son immediately restructured the keep, strengthened the curtain walls and added gatehouses, seven semi-circular towers and a barbican.

CONSTANT CONFLICT

The Percys were also engaged in constant warfare against the Scots or their monarchs, as a result of their Lancastrian loyalties, Roman Catholic beliefs, and their position as leaders of the northern barons. During the Wars of the Roses, Alnwick was one of three castles held by Lancastrian forces against Edward IV.

Alnwick Castle has been the principal seat of the Percy family since 1309

By 1750, Alnwick Castle had fallen into decay and Sir Hugh Smithson, later to become the 1st Duke of Northumberland, employed Robert Adams and Capability Brown to create extensive renovations.

 DID YOU KNOW?
Henry Percy's great-grandson Harry Hotspur featured in Shakespeare's play *Henry IV, Part One* because of his courage in battle.

England

WARKWORTH CASTLE

LOCATION: Castle Terrace, Warkworth, Northumberland, NE65 0UJ
DATE BUILT: c.1150
CASTLE STYLE: Norman
www.english-heritage.org.uk

The first castle at Warkworth was originally a wooden motte design, built just after the Norman Conquest. It was later developed into a masterwork of late medieval architecture.

SCOTTISH OWNERS

The Scottish king, David I gave the remains of the original motte and bailey castle to his son Prince Henry in 1139. Henry died in 1152 and the following year, his son became Malcolm IV of Scotland and inherited his father's lands. In 1157 though, Malcolm was forced to swear loyalty to the new king of England, Henry II, and surrender the lands he owned in northern England. Henry II granted Warkworth Castle to Roger FitzOsbern (see p.47), who immediately built a stone castle there.

An aerial view of Warkworth Castle

WEIRD AND WONDERFUL

As the northernmost English county on the border of England and Scotland, Northumberland (as Northumbria) was part of Scotland from 1139 to 1157.

ADVANCED DESIGN

In 1173, a Scottish raiding party easily captured Warkworth, so Roger's son Robert strengthened the castle's defences. His descendants continued improving the castle throughout the 13th century as they were involved in the fighting between

England and Scotland. The Scots besieged the castle twice in 1327, but were unsuccessful. In 1332, Edward III granted the castle to the powerful Percy family (who already owned nearby Alnwick Castle) to stand against the Scots.

The Percy family made big improvements to Warkworth, most notably the eight-towered keep in the late 14th century. The keep was an advanced design and provided impressive accommodation for the family. During the Civil War, the Scots occupied the castle in support of Parliament.

CONISBROUGH CASTLE

LOCATION: Doncaster, South Yorkshire, DN12 3BU
DATE BUILT: c.1180
CASTLE STYLE: Norman
www.conisbroughcastle.org.uk

Conisbrough Castle was built by Hamelin Plantagenet, an illegitimate half-brother of Henry II. It stands on the site of an earlier fortress which was held by William de Warenne and built around 1070.

A NATURAL MOTTE

The word 'Conisbrough' comes from the Anglo-Saxon *Cyningesburh*, meaning 'the defended burh of the king' and suggests that the area originally belonged to an Anglo-Saxon king. William, the first Earl de Warenne, was the son-in-law of William the Conqueror and had fought in the Battle of Hastings. William I gave him land in various parts of England, including Castle Acre in Norfolk and Lewes (p.15) in Sussex, but his main castle was Conisbrough. The original wooden motte and bailey was replaced by Hamelin, the 5th Earl de Warenne, in stone a century later.

NEW DESIGN

The enormous motte is a natural mound that supports the cylindrical keep, which is of a design not seen elsewhere in Britain. It resembles Mortemer Castle near Dieppe in France, also held by the Warenne family and probably designed by Hamelin Plantagenet. The keep has six wedge-shaped buttresses around it. With no windows or arrow slits, inside it is particularly dark and gloomy.

DID YOU KNOW?
Conisbrough Castle inspired Sir Walter Scott to write his epic novel *Ivanhoe*.

Conisbrough Castle was one of the first to have a non-rectangular keep

England

STONE CASTLES

Massive walls, soaring towers and deep moats; the impact of the great stone castles constructed across the land after the Norman Conquest was enormous. They frightened everyone outside the walls and protected those who lived inside.

SECURITY AND VISIBILITY

Once the Normans had shown that they had control of England they had more time and money to build stronger castles. However, stone castles did not 'evolve' from timber ones. They were built at the same time as each other, but stone castles developed further as methods of attack improved. Two main things were required: security and visibility, so natural elements, such as a high promontory above a river, were of foremost importance and the walls had to be used to best advantage.

WEIRD AND WONDERFUL

Cainhoe Castle in Bedfordshire was found abandoned after all its inhabitants died from the Black Death.

STRATEGIC LOCATIONS

As the ultimate sign of William the Conqueror's power over the English, the location of each castle was vital. To be prominent and commanding, they were built on the highest ground in the area, often overlooking rivers, above towns and roads or beside harbours. Several castles built in prime strategic locations could control the whole country.

DID YOU KNOW?

Spiral stairs in towers gave defenders an advantage. When attackers climbed up, the shape of the tower made them vulnerable to defenders above.

Castle builders learned new designs quickly. For instance, there was no point in simply making walls thicker and higher; an enemy who had reached a castle's base and was out of sight was quite safe as he could not be seen. One answer was to build a projecting area along the top of the wall with gaps in the floor (machicolations, see glossary p.93) through which missiles could be thrown or hot oil poured. Another solution was to build towers at short distances so defenders had a view and a field of fire.

UNDERMINING

Square stone keeps had a deadly weakness. Attackers dug tunnels beneath

Part of the outer walls of Dover Castle

them using timber props to hold them up. Then they set fire to the props and the weaker corners of the keeps collapsed, bringing down two of the walls and enabling attackers to storm the castle. This was called undermining and meant that round shell keeps with no corners became standard.

 WEIRD AND WONDERFUL
In 1136, a fire in Exeter Castle was extinguished with wine!

The weakest spot of any castle was its entrance so many doors were built on the first floor with wooden steps leading up to them. The steps were knocked away if an attack was about to happen. As methods of attacking and besieging castles gradually improved, defences had to change too.

 DID YOU KNOW?
Massive siege engines were used to attack stone built castles, including the ballista, mangonel, trebuchet and battering ram.

PREVENTING SIEGE
Medieval castle builders had few tools, but they made up for this in skilfulness. Wooden scaffolding was used and by the 13th century, new shaped keeps were built into curtain walls and barbicans provided further barriers.

The idea of concentric castles (see p.50) came from castles in the Byzantine Empire that had been seen by Crusaders.

The ruins of Berry Pomeroy Castle in Devon are said to be haunted

These prevented attackers from bringing siege weapons too

close and if invaders got through the outer wall, they found themselves exposed to further walls and an attack of arrows or hot oil from defenders.

Castles' purposes changed in the 14th century when there were fewer sieges and more fighting on battlefields. In addition, gunpowder had arrived in Europe, which was far stronger than any siege weapon. By the 15th century, traditional castles were becoming out of date. Feudalism (see p.66) was declining and fortified houses were becoming more popular.

 WEIRD AND WONDERFUL
Some attackers broke into castles through the sewers and climbed out of the latrines (toilets)!

Wales

Wales is often called the 'Land of Castles' because of the many sophisticated and commanding fortifications built there, from the Norman invasion until the 15th century.

A NETWORK OF CASTLES

Although the Normans built many castles in Wales, the most magnificent were those built by Edward I towards the end of the 13th century when castle architecture reached a golden age. After crushing a Welsh rebellion in 1278 Edward began planning a network of massive castles across the North West Welsh coast, enabling his lords to watch over and control the local people. This extremely expensive and time-consuming operation created a massive power-base for the English king.

1. Chepstow
2. Cardiff
3. Pembroke
4. Kidwelly
5. Criccieth
6. Caerphilly
7. Carew
8. Flint
9. Denbigh
10. Caernarfon
11. Harlech
12. Conwy
13. Beaumaris
14. Carreg Cennen

CHEPSTOW CASTLE

 LOCATION: Bridge St, Chepstow, Gwent NP16 5EY
DATE BUILT: 1067
CASTLE STYLE: Originally a stone motte and bailey
www.chepstow.co.uk

On its mound above the River Wye, Chepstow Castle was one of the first stone castles ever built in Britain. It was built in 1067, just months after William the Conqueror had invaded England.

DRAMATIC LOCATION

The area around Chepstow was of great strategic importance and William I ordered one of his best generals, William FitzOsbern, to build a castle there in order to control the Welsh Marches. FitzOsbern, the newly created Earl of Hereford, built the castle on a ridge where cliffs dropped down to the River Wye on one side and a deep valley fell away on another. The large rectangular keep and curtain walls included bands of red tiles, probably taken from a ruined Roman fort.

Despite several methods of medieval defence Chepstow was damaged during the Civil War

FOUR BAILEYS

Around 1190, Chepstow Castle passed by marriage to the great soldier William Marshal, Earl of Pembroke, who immediately began modernising the defences with stronger curtain walls on the vulnerable east side and had towers set into them. The remodelling was a huge undertaking, and was continued after Marshal's death by his five sons. By the time the last son died in 1246, the entire castle had been changed. After 1270, one of Edward I's most powerful barons, Roger Bigod, seventh Earl of Norfolk, added further buildings.

With its four baileys, Chepstow Castle shows the development of medieval defence methods. It was also refortified after being besieged during the Civil War with Parliamentary cannon in 1648.

 DID YOU KNOW?
Lawyer and politician Henry Marten played a leading role in organising Charles I's trial and execution. After the restoration of the monarchy, he was imprisoned at Chepstow Castle until his death.

CARDIFF CASTLE

LOCATION: Castle Street, Cardiff CF10 3RB
DATE BUILT: c.1081
CASTLE STYLE: Originally Norman motte and bailey
www.cardiffcastle.com

Beginning as a Roman fort built in about AD55 and continuing with the construction of a Norman keep over 1,000 years later, Cardiff Castle has had a long and bloody history.

STRATEGIC POSITION

The Romans located their fort near the meeting of the River Taff with the Bristol Channel. The location was of huge strategic value; as well as being on the meeting of important waterways it was also on the main routes between the settlements of Caerleon and Carmarthen.

After the Norman Conquest, William the Conqueror had a timber and earth motte and bailey castle built on the western side of the Roman fort. The Norman builders used some of the Roman stonework in their castle and surrounded it with a deep moat. In 1081 William gave the castle to Robert Fitzhamon along with the title 'Lord of Gloucester'.

12-SIDED STONE TOWER

In 1107, Fitzhamon was succeeded by his daughter Mabel who married Robert Fitzroy, the illegitimate son of Henry I. In 1122, Fitzroy was given the titles of Earl of Gloucester and Lord of Glamorgan and he replaced the wooden keep of Cardiff Castle with a 12-sided stone tower, which helped to protect it against the Welsh rebellions of 1183 and 1184.

Cardiff Castle's original keep was built in the 12th century

 DID YOU KNOW?
Fitzroy imprisoned his uncle, Robert Curthose, the rightful heir to the throne, at Cardiff from 1126 until his death in 1134.

CHANGING ARCHITECTURE

In 1776, the estate passed to the Earl of Bute. Employing architect Henry Holland and landscape artist 'Capability' Brown, the new earl made many alterations. In 1865, the third Marquess of Bute employed architect William Burges to remodel the castle in a Gothic Revival style, leaving the Norman keep intact.

PEMBROKE CASTLE

LOCATION: Pembroke, Pembrokeshire SA71 4LA
DATE BUILT: 1093
CASTLE STYLE: Originally Norman motte and bailey
www.pembroke-castle.co.uk

The first castle on this site was constructed in 1093 on a bend of the River Pembroke. Nearly 100 years later the castle passed to William Marshal who erected a massive stone tower.

DOMINATING TOWER

At the end of the 11th century, the Norman earl, Roger de Montgomery, built an earthwork motte and bailey castle in a corner of Wales on a site that had probably been occupied by the Romans.

In 1189, the powerful William Marshal (who became Regent to the infant Henry III) became Earl of Pembroke and the castle passed into his hands. He replaced the wooden castle with new stone buildings, including a massive four storey keep topped by an unusual stone dome.

The outer bailey, towers and gatehouse were gradually added by each of Marshal's five sons.

HENRY VII

After a series of different owners Henry VI gave the castle to his half-brother Jasper Tudor in 1452. Five years later, during the Wars of the Roses, Jasper's widowed sister-in-law, 15 year old Margaret Tudor, gave birth to a son at Pembroke – the future Henry VII.

IF YOU LIKED THIS...

Visit Richmond Castle in North Yorkshire, believed to be one of the oldest stone-built castles surviving today, or Beeston Castle with its natural defences.

SEVEN-WEEK SIEGE

At the start of the English Civil War, Pembroke chose to fight on the side of Parliament. The castle was besieged by Royalist troops but was saved by Parliamentary reinforcements. By the end of the war however, it had changed sides and Cromwell besieged it for seven weeks, eventually capturing it and ordering its destruction.

Pembroke Castle is built on a high ridge

CONCENTRIC CASTLES

One of the first people to build concentric castles in Britain was Edward I, through his chief architect and builder, Master James of St George. Concentric castles were easily defended by a relatively small number of men, providing an advantage in battle.

THE FIRST CONCENTRIC CASTLE

With at least two curtain walls and no central keep, all parts of concentric castles were important. Beaumaris Castle in North Wales (see p.64), although unfinished, is considered the ultimate concentric castle, but the first concentric castle was Caerphilly Castle in Gwent (see p.54), built not by Edward I, but by a rich lord, Gilbert de Clare.

 DID YOU KNOW?
Concentric castles were always built on land containing a well or a spring so that fresh water was readily available.

LATEST TECHNOLOGY

Concentric castles were based on three elements: an inner curtain wall with identical towers at regular intervals (this replaced the keep of former castles); an outer curtain wall that encircled the inner wall; and a strong gatehouse.

There were sometimes more than two curtain walls; the wall on the outside was also the smallest in height to allow the defenders to see approaching enemies. The curtain wall nearest to the castle was the highest, giving defenders the

Kenilworth's ruins date from the 12th to 16th centuries

maximum height advantage over anyone attempting to attack. Round towers in the walls did not have corners that might collapse if they were undermined (see p.44). Concentric curtain walls were usually between 2 and 6 metres (6 and 20 feet) thick.

Barbicans were built next to the gatehouses, which usually contained at least one portcullis, while crenellations or battlements provided a fighting platform for the defenders of the castle. Moats were usually dug around the whole castle and all of Edward I's castles had direct access to rivers or the sea, enabling boats to deliver supplies easily.

DID YOU KNOW?

White plaster, made from quicklime, sand, water and horsehair, coated both the inner and outer walls of most British concentric castles.

DEFENCE AGAINST REBELLION

Edward I probably met Master James of St George on his return from the Crusades. In 1278, after the first Welsh rebellion, Edward commissioned Master James to build four massive concentric castles, mightier than any castles that had been built before. More castles were built after the second Welsh rebellion of 1282 and new towns were built within fortified walls.

WEIRD AND WONDERFUL

When 'relaxing', knights entered jousts; mock battles where they galloped at each other in armour with lances. Many were killed during this entertaining spectator sport.

PREVENTING SIEGE

Concentric castles were bigger than previous castles, with thicker, stronger and higher walls, while the interiors were usually more comfortable. Outer curtain walls protected inner walls from siege engines, while inner walls and their towers allowed flanking fire from crossbows. The towers also served as platforms for trebuchets and other defensive weapons.

In essence, concentric castles made sieges far more difficult, but they had two main weaknesses. They were extremely costly

Piel Castle on Piel Island in Cumbria is a concentric castle

and time-consuming to build, requiring a lot of expensive materials. As they became more sophisticated, larger numbers of workers and greater building skills were needed. Labourers and craftsmen came from all over Britain.

It was not unusual to have over 2,000 men working on one castle, which would generally take several years to build. For instance, the castles of Conwy (see p.62), Caernarfon (see p.60) and Harlech (see p.61) had an average of 2,500 workers each. At any one time during its building, Beaumaris (see p.64) had approximately 3,500 men working on it. However, once Edward moved on to Scotland towards the end of his reign, the money he had available was running low and his extravagant castle-building was severely reduced.

IF YOU LIKED THIS...

Kenilworth Castle in the West Midlands and Dover Castle on England's south coast are two English concentric castles worth visiting.

KIDWELLY CASTLE

LOCATION: 5 Castle Street, Kidwelly, Carmarthenshire SA17 5BQ
DATE BUILT: 1106
CASTLE STYLE: Originally timber motte and bailey
http://cadw.wales.gov.uk

Kidwelly Castle was built on the estuary of the River Gwendraeth in South West Wales in 1106 by Roger, Bishop of Salisbury and Justiciar of England, to defend the road to the west of the country.

NATURAL STRUCTURE

Kidwelly's crescent shape developed from the original 12th century Norman timber motte and bailey castle that followed the natural geography of the land, with the river on one side and a deep arc-shaped ditch on the other.

Despite these natural defences, it wasn't a successful stronghold as it fell to the Welsh several times in its earliest years.

In the 1270s and early 1280s, the brothers Payn and Patrick de Chaworth transformed Kidwelly into a great stone concentric castle, with a square inner ward and cylindrical and semi-circular towers.

Kidwelly Castle was built in a crescent shape

DID YOU KNOW?

In 1136, Gwenllian, the wife of Gruffudd ap Rhys, Lord of Deheubarth, was killed in battle as she led Welsh forces against the castle.

INDEPENDENT GATEHOUSE

In 1291, Edward I gave Kidwelly Castle to his nephew, Henry, Earl of Lancaster, by arranging his marriage to the Kidwelly heiress. Henry immediately began adding further improvements, following the designs of Edward's mighty castles in Wales. He constructed an outer curtain wall, chapel tower, comfortable living accommodation and two gatehouses.

The largest gatehouse was still unfinished however over a century later, when in 1403 Owain Glyndwr's Welsh troops twice besieged the castle unsuccessfully. This massive gatehouse with portcullis, drawbridge, constable's lodgings above and dungeon pit below, was completed in 1422.

CRICCIETH CASTLE

LOCATION: Criccieth, Gwynedd LL52 0DP
DATE BUILT: 1230–80s
CASTLE STYLE: Enclosure castle
http://cadw.wales.gov.uk

In 1230 Llywelyn the Great of Gwynedd began building a castle on a rocky headland in a corner of Cardigan Bay. Making use of the natural defences, Llywelyn created a secure stronghold.

D-SHAPED TOWERS

Llywelyn fortified Criccieth Castle by cutting great ditches and building high banks around the plot. He then constructed two great D-shaped towers to protect the castle's vulnerable side.

Within 30 years, Llywelyn ap Gruffydd (Llywelyn the Last) had added a new outer curtain wall, gateway and a large two-storey rectangular tower.

In 1283, Criccieth was taken by the English forces and both Edward I and Edward II made improvements. The gatehouse had another storey added, the towers were remodelled and further buildings and another tower were built.

REBELLIONS AND SIEGES

In 1294, Madoc ap Llywelyn, a distant relation of Llywelyn ap Gruffydd, led a revolt against English rule. Criccieth, Harlech and Aberystwyth Castles were besieged, but supplies were delivered by sea to Criccieth and the inhabitants survived.

In 1404, however, the castle was not so fortunate, when it was besieged and captured by Owain Glyndwr. This time as Glyndwr was supported by the French navy, the approach of ships was prevented, so supplies never reached the castle inhabitants and they were forced to surrender. Glyndwr and his men robbed and burned the castle, leaving it in ruins.

 IF YOU LIKED THIS...
Try visiting Beeston Castle in Cheshire or Montgomery Castle in Shropshire.

Criccieth was destroyed by Owain Glyndwr in 1404

Wales

CAERPHILLY CASTLE

LOCATION: The Twyn, Caerphilly CF83 1JD
DATE BUILT: 1268–71
CASTLE STYLE: Medieval concentric
http://cadw.wales.gov.uk

The first concentric castle to be built in Britain, Caerphilly is one of the largest fortresses in Europe and represents the most advanced castle building developments of its time.

REVOLUTIONARY DESIGN

Caerphilly Castle is the largest castle in Wales and the second largest in Britain. It was an entirely new building which Gilbert de Clare raised between 1268 and 1271, mainly to reinforce his control of the area and to defend the land from Llywelyn ap Gruffydd.

Stretching over a 30 acre location, Caerphilly had extensive water defences and strong curtain walls and each of the towers and gatehouses was made to be able to stand independently if necessary.

WEIRD AND WONDERFUL

According to legend Caerphilly has many ghosts, including Gilbert de Clare's beautiful French wife Alice, known as the 'Green Lady', who died after Gilbert murdered her lover.

HUGH LE DESPENSER

In 1317, Hugh le Despenser became Lord of Glamorgan and Caerphilly Castle through his marriage to Eleanor, Gilbert de Clare's eldest daughter. As the weak King Edward II's favourite, Hugh became extremely powerful, greedy – and hated. In 1326, the king's estranged wife Queen Isabella and others marched to Caerphilly where Edward and Hugh were in hiding and besieged the castle.

Further influential figures made slight enhancements to the castle, but at the end of the 15th century Caerphilly was no longer useful as either a home or a defence. After the Civil War, Cromwell ordered it to be slighted (destroyed) and the damage caused resulted in one tower leaning at an alarming angle over the lake.

Caerphilly Castle's inner west gatehouse

Wales

CAREW CASTLE

LOCATION: Pembroke, SA70 8SL
DATE BUILT: c.1270
CASTLE STYLE: Norman rectangular castle
www.pembrokeshirecoast.org.uk

Standing on a rock overlooking a rare tidal mill where the River Carew enters the sea, Carew Castle is an interesting combination of a strong medieval fortress and a grand Tudor mansion.

In 1507 the last medieval tournament was held at Carew Castle

THE DE CAREW FAMILY

In 1095 a Norman knight, Gerald de Windsor, received Carew as part of his wife's dowry (wedding gift). He built an earthwork castle with a stone tower on the land. His descendants adopted the name 'de Carew' and in around 1270, Sir Nicholas de Carew rebuilt the castle entirely in stone, adding a great hall and two drum towers.

DID YOU KNOW?
An ornately carved 4 metre (13 feet) stone cross near to Carew Castle is a memorial to a Celtic king who died in battle in 1035.

THE TUDORS

By 1480, the de Carews sold their castle to Rhys ap Thomas who was part of the Lancastrian army supporting the Tudors. Rewarded by the future Henry VII with money and later lands and a knighthood, Rhys spent huge amounts of money converting Carew Castle into a magnificent home with a grand hall and porch.

The Royal allegiance changed however in 1531, when Henry VIII had Rhys' grandson, Rhys ap Gruffydd, executed for treason.

Badly damaged in the Civil War, Carew Castle was abandoned in 1685.

EDWARD I AND CASTLE BUILDING

The castles built by Edward I represent his most impressive and lasting legacy. Between 1276 and 1295, he developed a new style of military architecture in an effort to control and unite Britain.

IRON RING

All of Edward's castles were built in strategic locations with access to the sea or rivers so that provisions could be delivered if they were attacked. Many were raised in what became known as Edward's 'iron ring'. Each castle was within a day's march of another, creating a chain of protection.

Most of the castles featured the latest developments in castle building that Edward had probably seen in Constantinople while on his Crusade to the Holy Land from 1271 to 1272. His formidable ring of castles was medieval Europe's most ambitious building project.

Cream-coloured bands of stone dominate Caernarfon's walls

DID YOU KNOW?

Eleanor of Castile, Edward I's beloved wife, is believed to have been the first person to put carpets on the floor in her castle bedrooms, rather than hang them on the walls or over tables.

TWO PHASES

Edward's Welsh castles were built in two phases. Flint (see p.58), Builth, Rhuddlan and Aberystwyth were built after the first Welsh war of 1277, when he fought to suppress Llywelyn ap Gruffydd. By 1258, Llywelyn had gained control of most of central and northern Wales and in calling himself the Prince of Wales, wanted to rule there. After his defeat in 1278, Llywelyn signed a peace treaty, but five years later, he rebelled again. So in 1282, Edward invited the master mason James of St George to build more castles in Wales, resulting in Conwy (see p.62), Caernarfon (see p.60) and Beaumaris (see p.64).

WEIRD AND WONDERFUL

Edward's castle-building in Wales involved thousands of workers over a 25 year period and cost millions of pounds.

DID YOU KNOW?
Edward II was born in Caernarfon Castle in 1284 and named Prince of Wales there in 1301, beginning the tradition of that title going to the heir to the throne. This tradition continues today.

SHARED FEATURES

Edward's castles had several features in common, but they were not identical. Each was designed to take advantage of the location and any natural or pre-built elements. Instead of motte and bailey structures, castle walls and towers were built in concentric circles, making it more difficult for invaders to reach the inner part of the castle. The round towers or shell keeps (see p.50) gave defenders a broader field of fire.

Edward also built or remodelled some English castles. Between 1275 and 1285, he extended and strengthened the Tower of London with a new curtain wall, two huge gatehouses and a barbican which controlled access to a series of bridges.

WEIRD AND WONDERFUL
During Edward I's reign, his castles were decorated with bright bold colours. Gold was a particularly popular paint colour as it signified wealth.

THE CULT OF KING ARTHUR

Edward was a strong king. Tall and powerful, one of his nicknames was Edward Longshanks. He was an expert warrior, skilled general, great politician

Edward I was a shrewd castle builder

and faithful husband, but he was also hot-tempered, ambitious, overly proud and dishonest. He identified with the legendary King Arthur who was supposed to have united England, Scotland and Wales during his rule. Edward had similar ambitions.

The Arthurian legends were particularly popular at the time and had become quite a cult in Wales. There had been associations with Merlin for centuries at Caernarfon, which is probably why Edward built a castle there in 1283. When Edward had a new castle built, he also usually had a new town constructed at the same time. Following the style of bastides built in France, or burghs built in Scotland, these new towns helped Edward confirm his control across Wales.

IMPREGNABILITY

The effectiveness of Edward's castle-based defence strategy was put to the test in 1294. A distant relative of Llywelyn (who Edward had defeated in 1278), Madog ap Llywelyn, led a rebellion when Edward was about to travel to France. Edward turned and led his troops to Wales. All of his castles survived the attack and the revolt was crushed.

FLINT CASTLE

LOCATION: Flint, Flintshire CH6 5PE
DATE BUILT: 1277–84
CASTLE STYLE: Enclosure castle
http://cadw.wales.gov.uk

The first of the castles built during Edward I's campaign to conquer Wales in 1277, Flint stands on a promontory overlooking the estuary of the River Dee. It took approximately 2,300 men nine years to complete.

CORNER KEEP

Flint Castle features a rectangular enclosure with four round towers at each corner. One of the towers – the keep – was larger than the others. Additional strong walls, ditches and a moat gave it extra protection. Ordered by the king, building work began in the summer of 1277 under Richard L'Engenour, a master mason who became the Mayor of Chester in 1304.

In 1282, while it was still under construction, Flint Castle withstood a siege led by Dafydd ap Gruffydd, brother of Llywelyn ap Gruffydd. The Welsh besieged the castle again in 1294 during the rebellion of Madog ap Llywelyn, but the castle's constable set fire to the fortress to prevent its capture by the Welsh. Massive repairs were undertaken afterwards.

Even in ruins Flint Castle looks imposing

HENRY BOLINGBROKE

In 1399, Henry Bolingbroke captured Richard II at Flint. The king was forced to return to London and to abdicate in favour of Henry who became King Henry IV. Richard was eventually taken to Pontefract Castle in Yorkshire where he was murdered. During the Civil War, Flint Castle was occupied by the Royalists, but in 1647 the Parliamentarians successfully besieged and then destroyed it.

WEIRD AND WONDERFUL

Dafydd ap Gruffydd was the first person known to have been tried for high treason against the king. He was executed by being hung, drawn and quartered.

DENBIGH CASTLE

LOCATION: Denbigh LL16 3NB
DATE BUILT: c.1282
CASTLE STYLE: Enclosure castle
http://cadw.wales.gov.uk

Built on the site of an earlier stronghold, on the estuary of the River Clwyd, Denbigh Castle was part of Edward I's ambitious building plans in Wales. 'Denbigh' means 'little fort' in Welsh.

ROYAL CHARTER

The current Denbigh Castle was built on the site of a former Welsh stronghold held by Dafydd ap Gruffydd. After Dafydd's defeat in 1282, one of the king's successful military leaders, Henry de Lacy, Earl of Lincoln, was granted the lordship and estate. Before building the castle, de Lacy removed all traces of the Welsh fort. He was also granted a Royal Charter to build a fortified town (bastide) at the same time as the castle.

Denbigh Castle helped Edward I achieve the Statute of Wales

DID YOU KNOW?
In 1308, de Lacy's 15 year old son Edmund fell to his death in Denbigh Castle's well and consequently his father lost all interest in the castle.

OCTAGONAL TOWERS

It is thought that the king and his architect, James of St George, helped de Lacy with the planning of Denbigh Castle, which was built over two phases. The first, in 1282, saw the construction of part of the curtain wall, towers, gatehouse and the new town walls. The second phase was in 1295, after the castle had been attacked and taken by Madog ap Llywelyn in 1294 and then

recaptured by de Lacy. In the second phase, the curtain wall was refortified and three octagonal towers, a drawbridge, great hall and postern gate were added.

A Royalist stronghold during the Civil War, Denbigh Castle was eventually besieged for six months and destroyed by Parliamentarian forces.

IF YOU LIKED THIS...
Visit Chirk Castle in Wrexham, another of Edward I's Welsh castles.

CAERNARFON CASTLE

 LOCATION: Castle Ditch, Caernarfon, Gwynedd LL55 2AY
DATE BUILT: 1283
CASTLE STYLE: Concentric castle
http://cadw.wales.gov.uk

Often described as Edward I's finest Welsh castle, Caernarfon was begun in 1283 after Llywelyn ap Gruffydd's second uprising. Work continued on the castle until 1323, but it was never finished.

BANDS OF COLOUR

Built in bands of coloured stone, reputedly based on the walls of Constantinople (that protected the capital of the Byzantine Empire), Caernarfon Castle stands on the banks of the River Seiont. Originally the Romans had a fort there and in 1073, a motte and bailey castle was built on the site by a Norman earl, but the castle was in possession of the Welsh by 1115. Edward I wanted Caernarfon to be a military stronghold, a seat of government and a royal palace.

In 1284, the future Edward II was born at Caernarfon, which Edward I hoped would create a bond with the Welsh people. Ten years later, Madog ap Llywelyn led a rebellion and destroyed the castle. Recaptured the following year, the castle entered its second phase of building. The defences were strengthened with further curtain walls, a drawbridge and six portcullises.

 WEIRD AND WONDERFUL

Caernarfon was Edward I's most expensive castle, costing approximately £27,000 — in today's terms that would be about £40,000,000.

THE ACTS OF UNION

Edward I's descendants did not use Caernarfon as a royal palace as he had planned, but it remained a military stronghold and resisted Owain Glyndwr's sieges in 1403 and 1404. When the Tudors took the throne, hostilities between the English and Welsh eased. The Acts of Union were passed during Henry VIII's reign and the need for castles in Wales diminished.

Caernarfon was built in a figure of eight with a series of towers

HARLECH CASTLE

LOCATION: Harlech, Gwynedd LL46 2YH
DATE BUILT: 1283
CASTLE STYLE: Concentric castle
http://cadw.wales.gov.uk

Edward I hired Master James of St George to design Harlech Castle, which was built to secure the area of Snowdonia. It was constructed as part of a series of castles along with Conwy, Caernarfon and Beaumaris.

STRONG DEFENCES

Harlech Castle was built between 1283 and 1290. Protected on one side by high cliffs and on the other by a deep moat, it was one of the four massive castles built rapidly by Edward I in his second stage of castle construction. A concentric design with immense inner walls and round corner towers, it was surrounded by lower outer walls and dominated by a huge gatehouse with two D-shaped towers.

In 1294, 37 men stationed in Harlech Castle resisted an assault by Madog ap Llywelyn, but in 1404 it fell to Owain Glyndwr after a long siege. Glyndwr lived in the castle for four years until it was retaken by an army led by Harry of Monmouth, Prince of Wales; the future Henry V.

Harlech Castle's battlements rise impressively above Tremadog Bay

SEVEN-YEAR SIEGE

In 1468, during the Wars of the Roses, Harlech was the last Lancastrian fortress to surrender. It had withstood a seven-year siege, which began when the Yorkist Edward IV was crowned and as the longest siege in British history, it inspired the song *Men of Harlech*. During the Civil War, Harlech was the last Royalist stronghold to fall to the Parliamentarians, who subsequently destroyed it.

DID YOU KNOW?

In 1286, the workforce building Harlech Castle consisted of 546 general labourers, 115 quarriers, 30 blacksmiths, 22 carpenters and 227 stonemasons.

Wales

CONWY CASTLE

LOCATION: Rose Hill Street, Conwy LL32 8LD
DATE BUILT: 1283
CASTLE STYLE: Rectangular enclosure castle
http://cadw.wales.gov.uk

Another of Edward I's second phase of castles in Wales, Conwy Castle was built to fit a long thin rocky outcrop overlooking the estuary of the River Conwy.

EIGHT MASSIVE TOWERS

Edward had Conwy Castle constructed to replace Deganawy Castle which had been built by Henry III from 1245 and destroyed by Llywelyn ap Gruffydd in 1263. Conwy was also built to guard the entrance to the River Conwy. Taking an incredible five years to build, from 1283 to around 1287, Conwy was a vast enclosure divided into an inner and outer ward, with eight enormous round towers and two barbicans.

Thick 10 metre (30 feet) high curtain walls surround both the baileys and the castle's

irregular shape that follows its natural rock base, and so it could not be concentric. As well as being a strong fortress, Conwy was also a luxurious palace; the inner ward contained a magnificent Great Hall and other grand Royal apartments.

 WEIRD AND WONDERFUL

Conwy Castle was built on the site of the monastery of Aberconwy, which Edward I ordered to be moved elsewhere.

THE COSTLIEST CASTLE

While Conwy was being built, the town's defences were also constructed, with a series of high walls interspersed by 21 towers and three twin-towered gatehouses, but unusually, the castle itself had no gatehouse. Instead, the castle entrance featured a steep flight of winding stairs, a drawbridge and a gateway. The design and construction of the whole project was overseen by Master James of St George, using nearly 2,000 workmen.

ALMOST CAUGHT

Despite its tough defences, Conwy Castle relied heavily on the surrounding

A copy of one of Conwy's original stained glass windows

The colossal walls and towers of Conwy Castle are a great example of James of St George's designs

waterways for delivery of supplies. In 1294, Edward I arrived with a small force when Madog ap Llywelyn was leading his rebellion. As the river was exceptionally high, Conwy was cut off during the siege which lasted several months. Although supplies ran low, the castle inhabitants resisted capture.

 DID YOU KNOW?
Each of the eight huge towers of Conwy Castle are nearly 21 metres (70 feet) high and 9 metres (30 feet) in diameter with walls up to 4.6 metres (15 feet) thick.

THE BETRAYAL OF A KING
In 1399, the unpopular King Richard II met Henry Percy, the Earl of Northumberland at Conwy Castle to discuss his abdication. A week later, Richard surrendered to Henry Bolingbroke at Flint Castle agreeing to give up his crown if his life was spared. Briefly imprisoned in the Tower of London, he was transferred to Pontefract Castle, where he was murdered a few months later.

 IF YOU LIKED THIS...
Try visiting the ruins of Aberystwyth Castle, which was once considered the most imposing castle in Wales.

DECAY AND DESTRUCTION
During the Wars of the Roses, Edward IV ordered William Herbert, Earl of Pembroke to take control of Conwy Castle, but it became neglected and slowly fell into ruin. Nearly 200 years later, John Williams, the Archbishop of York and a Royalist, repaired the castle at his own expense. By 1655, an order was issued for Conwy Castle to be slighted. Now only its outer walls remain.

BEAUMARIS CASTLE

LOCATION: Castle Street, Beaumaris, Isle of Anglesey LL85 8AP

DATE BUILT: 1295

CASTLE STYLE: Concentric castle

http://cadw.wales.gov.uk

French for 'beautiful marsh', *Beau Mareys* or Beaumaris Castle was started in 1295, the last and largest of the castles built by Edward I in Wales. Although wonderfully designed it was never completed.

ADVANCED AND AMBITIOUS DESIGN

Abandoned before it was finished, Beaumaris Castle is nevertheless considered to be the most advanced and ambitious example of medieval military architecture in Britain.

 DID YOU KNOW?
While Beaumaris was being built Edward I ordered that the inhabitants of nearby Llanfaes be evicted from their homes and relocated to the far side of Anglesey.

The moat around Beaumaris was refreshed by the tide

Soon after Madog ap Llywelyn's uprising of 1294, Edward I ordered Master James of St George – 18 years after his first assignment in Britain – to build another larger castle, incorporating all the latest building developments he could. Built on an untouched coastal site on the island of Anglesey, Beaumaris gave Master James a free hand. It was constructed with two perfectly symmetrical rings of walling, flanking towers and defensive gatehouses surrounded by a wide moat. The gatehouses also included grand chambers.

BUILDING CEASES

By the time construction began, Welsh uprisings were less frequent, with the leaders of rebellions either dead or defeated. By 1298, Edward needed money for his Scottish campaigns and work on Beaumaris stopped. Edward I died in 1307 and Master James of St George died in 1309. Building recommenced from 1306, but never as intensely as before and by 1330, the castle was neglected and deteriorating, never achieving the importance Edward had planned for it, reflected in the fact that the Parliamentarians left Beaumaris alone during the Civil War.

CARREG CENNEN

 LOCATION: Trapp, Llandeilo, Carmarthenshire SA19 6UA
DATE BUILT: (current remains) c.1300
CASTLE STYLE: Enclosure castle
http://cadw.wales.gov.uk

Perched on top of a spectacular limestone crag, Carreg Cennen Castle is dramatically situated 100 metres above the Cennen valley. There was probably an earlier fortress on the site, but little evidence remains.

A STRATEGIC STRONGHOLD

The present Carreg Cennen Castle standing today was started in around 1300. Three sides of it were protected by steep cliffs and hills with a natural cave underneath. Although now ruined, Carreg Cennen was clearly a sophisticated and effective construction at the time it was built.

There are records of a castle being there from 1248. Since then the castle has been frequently attacked, captured and damaged in territorial uprisings and it was repaired and refortified many times. Eventually in 1277, Edward I seized control and in 1283 he gave it to one of his barons, John Giffard, the commander of the English troops when Llywelyn ap Gruffydd was killed. It is thought that Giffard built the present castle.

 WEIRD AND WONDERFUL
In the 11th century, Carreg Cennen was held by a Welsh prince, Rhys Fychan. He withstood attacks, but his mother gave the fort to the Normans because she hated her son.

Carreg Cennen withstood many attacks until it was demolished in 1462

ELABORATE BARBICAN

Skilfully adapted to the rocky surroundings, Carreg Cennen Castle consists of a rectangular enclosure featuring high curtain walls and different shaped towers, including a succession of pits, drawbridges, a great twin-towered gatehouse and an elaborate barbican. In 1403, Owain Glyndwr and his men attacked and damaged the castle, but failed to capture it. During the Wars of the Roses, it became a Lancastrian stronghold, but it was captured and demolished by the Yorkists in 1462.

FEUDAL SOCIETY

Castles developed as an essential part of the feudal system, which was William I's way of controlling the people. As soon as he took command of Britain, he rigidly organised the way society worked.

Jousting was a popular spectator sport during feudal times

PYRAMID OF IMPORTANCE

The feudal structure of society began in Europe in the ninth century, but was firmly established in Britain by the Normans after 1066. Based on the distribution of land in return for service, the division of society in the feudal system worked because everyone kept to their place. Like a pyramid, the monarch was at the top and the peasants or villeins were at the bottom.

DID YOU KNOW?
In 1215 King John was forced to sign the Magna Carta by powerful English barons. It was the first time in history that an English monarch had to obey the law.

SWEARING ALLEGIANCE

The king's rule was absolute; he ruled by the will of God and owned all the land in the country. He granted areas of land (fiefs) to the church and to the barons, giving permission to build castles or manor houses and to keep a private army. In return the barons had to swear allegiance to him, to attend councils, participate in ceremonies, welcome the royal court when it travelled around the country and supply the king with soldiers in time of war.

Barons granted some of their land to knights in return for the knights' protection and loyalty. Knights gave some of their land to freemen and peasants, villeins or serfs. In return, these lower orders had to work on the land, undertake all manual work and provide their lord with food. Peasants had few rights, but the whole system would have collapsed without these workers at the bottom of the system.

 DID YOU KNOW?
After the population fell drastically in the 14th century as a result of the Black Death, the few surviving peasants began to demand higher wages, which destroyed the feudal system.

BINDING OATHS

The feudal system relied on the oaths of fidelity and loyalty that everyone took. For instance, many took part in acts of homage and fealty (swearing loyalty) during solemn ceremonies, which were meant to be binding for life. The vassal (person swearing loyalty) would kneel before his lord, bareheaded and without weapons and repeat an oath such as 'I promise on my faith that I will in future be faithful to [name of king, baron or knight] and will observe my homage to him completely against all persons in good faith and without deceit.'

ASSERTING POWER

Although it was difficult, occasionally it was possible to move up the ranks in the feudal system. Most peasants accepted their circumstances, but a few hoped to become freemen and many knights sought to be nobles. A knight could, for instance, earn more money or land through displays of bravery or military success and from that he might be invited to build or lease a castle. Once that was achieved, he could be given a title and become one of the lords or barons just below the king in rank. Throughout the castle-building period

many powerful nobles aspired to be king, which was often why the castles were built in the first place!

Castles were essential to the feudal system because they were so striking and authoritative and they asserted the lord's power over his estate, keeping his vassals in check and warning others away. Castles provided a base for nobles to govern and allocate their land.

 WEIRD AND WONDERFUL
In 1086 William I ordered a survey to find out what every English person owned and owed in taxes. Hated by the people, it became known the 'Domesday Book'.

 IF YOU LIKED THIS...
Read *The Canterbury Tales* by Chaucer. The characters depict different levels of feudal society including a knight and a plowman.

Dover Castle was used to enforce the feudal system

Scotland

Soon after they had made their authority known in England and Wales, many Norman barons travelled to Scotland and began building castles, but on the whole, Scottish castles were built by the Scots themselves.

NORMAN INFLUENCE

David I of Scotland, who was brother-in-law to William the Conqueror's youngest son, Henry I of England, invited Norman barons to build castles in Scotland. Over the course of the 12th century the Normans who moved there introduced the feudal system to Scotland, building motte and bailey castles, as they had done in England. The Norman influence spread quickly and within that century, the Scottish ruling class almost wholly originated from the Normans. Many Scottish names such as Bruce, Ramsay, Fraser, Ogilvie, Montgomery, Sinclair, Pollock, Douglas and Gordon, derive from the Normans.

RISE IN CASTLE BUILDING

Not all castles were built on new sites. Some important royal castles, including Edinburgh, were built on rock outcrops that had been inhabited since the Bronze

Age 2,000 years earlier. Stone castles were rare in Scotland until the 13th century and after that, most were still simple towers.

By the end of the 13th century though, the instability of many areas of Scotland and the border region (due mainly to wars led by Edward I) led to a dramatic increase in more sophisticated castle building. As the massive stone castles were expensive and took a lot of workers and a long time to build, locations in Scotland were chosen extremely carefully, to ensure that they were particularly powerful and intimidating.

COMPETING WITH ROYALTY

A lot of problems arose in Scotland because many Scottish kings inherited the crown as infants, such as David II and Mary, Queen of Scots.

Kilchurn Castle on Loch Awe

Conflicts arose among the influential barons as jealousies and power struggles intensified. A large number of families became more powerful and competed with royalty, declaring their importance by building great stone castles. Throughout the 15th century growing numbers of landowners (lairds) could afford to build their own mighty castles for protection and as a show of their strength.

STATUS AND PRESTIGE

During the 16th century, Scottish castles were designed with originality and innovation, but they became less like castles and more like private homes. After that, several lairds continued to build fortified homes that they called castles, adding some fortifications, but more often, separate forts filled with soldiers were built for defence.

1. Edinburgh	10. Urquhart
2. St Andrews	11. Glamis
3. Dunnottar	12. Stirling
4. Eilean Donan	13. Doune
5. Hermitage	14. Kilchurn
6. Duart	15. Culzean
7. Blair	16. Braemar
8. Dunvegan	17. Floors
9. Cawdor	18. Balmoral

Scotland

EDINBURGH CASTLE

LOCATION: Castlehill Edinburgh EH1 2NG
DATE BUILT: c.1130 but remains date from 16th century
CASTLE STYLE: Norman and 16th century
www.edinburghcastle.gov.uk

From its position on the top of an extinct volcano, Edinburgh Castle dominates the skyline of the city. Its history stretches back thousands of years, with human occupancy probably dating from the ninth century BC.

ROYAL RESIDENCE AND PRISON

The castle site thrived in the first and second century when Scotland was under Roman occupation. During that time, it was called Din Eidyn, meaning 'the stronghold of Eidyn'.

At the end of the 11th century, Malcolm II of Scotland built a castle there. From the start of the 12th century, the castle was used as a royal residence, a storehouse, sheriff's headquarters and as a prison.

Much damaged and often changing hands, most of Edinburgh Castle was rebuilt in stone in the 13th century before Edward I invaded and captured it in 1296. It was taken back by the Scots in 1314 and David II started rebuilding. By 1386, work began on a massive L-shaped tower house.

Edinburgh did not become the capital city until the reign of James III in the second half of the 15th century and, as befitting a fortress guarding its capital, the castle was rearranged with a new courtyard and a Great Hall.

DID YOU KNOW?

Mons Meg, Edinburgh's giant cannon, was given as a gift to James II in 1457 by his uncle Philip the Good, Duke of Burgundy.

MARY QUEEN OF SCOTS

In 1567, one year after Mary Queen of Scots had given birth to her son James in Edinburgh Castle, she married the Earl of Bothwell who was accused of murdering her husband. This triggered a rebellion by the Scottish nobles and Mary was forced to step down from the throne. She eventually escaped to England, but meanwhile, the keeper of Edinburgh Castle remained loyal to Mary and defiantly held the castle against Scotland's new Regent, James Douglas of Morton. 'The Lang Siege', as it became known, lasted from 1571 to 1573 and only ended when Morton sought assistance from England. Through a massive bombardment by cannons and other weapons, most of Edinburgh Castle was reduced to rubble. Reconstruction of the defences began almost immediately.

WEIRD AND WONDERFUL

In 1558, a stone cannonball was fired from Edinburgh Castle to celebrate the marriage of Mary Queen of Scots to the French Dauphin. It landed almost 3 kilometres (2 miles) away!

KING OF SCOTLAND AND ENGLAND

In 1603, when Elizabeth I died childless, James VI of Scotland was next in line to the throne, linking Scotland and England with one monarch. James VI of Scotland and I of England moved to London and returned to Scotland only once, in 1617. To welcome him, Edinburgh Castle was refurbished. In 1633, Charles I became the last sovereign to sleep in the castle just before he was crowned king of Scotland. After Charles I was beheaded, Oliver Cromwell set up his Scottish headquarters at Edinburgh and the castle survived as a military base. The last military action occurred there during the 1745 Jacobite Rising, when James Stuart (The Old Pretender) tried unsuccessfully to capture it.

DID YOU KNOW?

The earliest surviving building of Edinburgh Castle is a small chapel, probably built by David I at the beginning of the 12th century and dedicated to his mother, who was canonised as St Margaret after his death.

In the 11th century Edinburgh Castle was known as the Castle of the Maidens

Scotland

ST ANDREWS CASTLE

 LOCATION: North Street, St Andrews, Fife KY16 9AR
DATE BUILT: c.1200
CASTLE STYLE: Norman
www.historic-scotland.gov.uk

On a rocky crag overlooking a small beach, St Andrews Castle was once the official residence of Scotland's leading bishops. The first castle on the site, destroyed during the Wars of Independence, dates from around 1200.

BISHOPS' PALACE

In the 10th century, the bishops of St Andrews were given responsibility for the Scottish Church and by 1200 their first castle was built. In 1296, Edward I took the castle but it was retaken by the Scots in 1314. The English recaptured and reinforced it, but after a successful three-week siege in 1336, the Scots destroyed it as a deterrent to the English.

At the end of the 14th century, Bishop Trail rebuilt St Andrews Castle as a powerful fortification. In 1445 James III was born there, while below ground the castle's 'bottle dungeon' was a notorious prison.

St Andrews Castle was subject to many attacks before it fell to ruin in the 17th century

 ## WEIRD AND WONDERFUL

Prisoners were dropped through the narrow neck opening of St Andrews' 'bottle dungeon', where they fell into a large, dark, cold pit under the castle.

THE GREAT SIEGE

In March 1546, the Archbishop of St Andrews, Cardinal Beaton, burnt the Protestant preacher George Wishart in front of the castle walls. The Cardinal was unpopular because he was against the marriage of the Protestant English Prince Edward to the Catholic Mary Queen of Scots. A group of Protestant lairds gained access to the castle, murdered Beaton and occupied the castle.

Immediately, a siege was ordered by the Scottish Regent, James Hamilton and in 1546, his men began mining beneath the castle, aiming to weaken the foundations, but the defenders successfully countermined it.

DUNNOTTAR CASTLE

LOCATION: Stonehaven, Kincardineshire AB39 2TL
DATE BUILT: c.1200
CASTLE STYLE: L-plan
www.dunnottarcastle.co.uk

Standing on a flat-topped cliff jutting into the North Sea, Dunnottar Castle is joined to the mainland by a narrow strip of land. Almost completely surrounded by the sea, it appears both enchanting and forbidding at once.

DUN FOITHER

The site of Dunnottar Castle was inhabited by the Picts from 5,000BC to AD700. The name Dunnottar derives from the Pictish words *Dun foither* which mean 'fort on the shelving slope'. Little is known about the castle's early history, but William the Lion used an earlier construction as an administrative centre in the 12th century.

In 1297, William Wallace led the Scots to victory over the English at the castle. In 1336 Edward III seized it, but within months the Regent of Scotland, Sir Andrew Moray, recaptured it.

DID YOU KNOW?
Dunnottar Castle was used by Franco Zeffirelli as the backdrop for his celebrated 1990 film version of Shakespeare's *Hamlet*.

THE EARLS MARISCHAL

By the end of the 14th century, Dunnottar had become home to one of the most powerful families in Scotland, the Earls Marischal. The first earl, Sir William Keith, rebuilt Dunnottar Castle on the promontory, 49 metres (160 feet) above

Spectacular Dunnottar Castle at dawn

the sea. It became the stronghold of the Keith clan and over time, they turned Dunnottar Castle into one of Scotland's most impressive residences.

During Cromwell's invasion of Scotland, the Scottish crown jewels were stored there, but in 1651, Cromwell's army laid siege to the castle. After eight months they broke through, but by then, the crown jewels had been smuggled away.

IF YOU LIKED THIS...
Visit Castle Stalker, situated on an island in Loch Laich in Argyll.

Scotland

EILEAN DONAN CASTLE

LOCATION: Dornie, Kyle of Lochalsh IV40 8DX
DATE BUILT: 1220
CASTLE STYLE: Medieval
www.eileandonancastle.com

Standing proudly on a small, rocky island at the junction of three lochs, Eilean Donan Castle, joined to the mainland by an arched bridge, is a 20th century reconstruction of an early 13th century fortress.

VIKING RAIDERS

Also known as Donan Castle, it is thought that this castle was named after the sixth century Irish saint, Bishop Donan, who went to Scotland in around AD580. The original castle was built in 1220 for Alexander II as defence against Viking raiders.

By the end of that century, it had become the stronghold of the Mackenzies of Kintail and in 1511, the Macraes, as protectors of the Mackenzies, became the hereditary Constables of the castle.

WEIRD AND WONDERFUL

The Macraes had a habit of displaying the heads of their enemies on the battlements of the castle.

BOMBARDMENT AND DESTRUCTION

Over the centuries Eilean Donan Castle expanded and contracted in size. The early 13th century castle had towers and a curtain wall that covered nearly the whole island. By the end of the 14th century, it was reduced to about a fifth of its original size.

During the Jacobite Rebellion of 1715, the Macraes supported the exiled Prince of Wales, son of the deposed James II of England, James VII of Scotland. Four years later, 46 Spanish soldiers who supported the Jacobites occupied the castle, but the English learned of this and Royal Navy ships bombarded the castle walls, pounding it to pieces.

It lay neglected until it was reconstructed in the 20th century by a descendant of the Macrae family.

Surrounded by three lochs, Eilean Donan was once used as a refuge by Robert the Bruce

HERMITAGE CASTLE

LOCATION: Near Newcastleton, Scottish Borders TD9 0LU
DATE BUILT: c.1240
CASTLE STYLE: Motte and bailey
www.historic-scotland.gov.uk

Surrounded by moors on the border, where it was frequently involved in many conflicts, Hermitage Castle served as the 'guardhouse of the bloodiest valley in Britain' and still appears bleak and sinister.

UNCEASING INSTABILITY

Built over several centuries, Hermitage Castle's position close to the English border made it appealing to the rulers of both countries. The area was a place of constant turmoil and instability and Hermitage Castle changed hands many times.

The first wooden motte and bailey castle was built by Sir Nicholas de Soules in about 1240, but after his death, de Soules' son William was evicted following his involvement in a conspiracy to kill Robert the Bruce.

Hermitage Castle has a violent and volatile history

DID YOU KNOW?

In 1566, Mary Queen of Scots rode 50 miles (80km) in one day, from Jedburgh to Hermitage Castle and back, to visit her wounded lover, the fourth Earl of Bothwell.

STRATEGIC POSITION

In 1338, the castle was captured by Sir William Douglas, who disposed of his enemy, Sir Alexander Ramsay, by leaving him to starve at the bottom of a pit. When Sir William's kinsman, also William,

the first Earl of Douglas, took control later that century, he built the first stone castle, including an enormous tower. Four smaller sandstone towers were added to the corners and finally a rectangular wing was built.

Gunports were added in around 1540, as the castle continued to be passed from hand to hand because of its strategic position. Eventually, the castle's military importance lessened and by the 17th century it was abandoned. The atmospheric and windswept ruins are alleged to be haunted.

DUART CASTLE

LOCATION: Craignure, Isle of Mull, PA64 6AP
DATE BUILT: c.1250
CASTLE STYLE: Tower house
www.duartcastle.com

Originally built for the MacDougalls of Dunollie in around 1250 to guard the navigation route of the Sound of Mull, Duart Castle became the seat of the Maclean chiefs at the end of the 14th century.

BLACK POINT

The name Duart comes from the Gaelic words *Dub Ard* meaning 'Black Point'. In about 1367, Lady Mary MacDonald, the daughter of the Lord of the Isles, married the clan chief, Lachlan Lubanach Maclean, and was given land on Mull and Duart as a dowry.

Over the next 20 years, Lachlan added considerably to the castle defences, in particular the Great Keep or Tower House on the outside of the original curtain wall. The Macleans later added to the castle, including vaulted cellars, a hall and a two-storey gatehouse.

SURRENDER

Duart Castle was protected by its exceptionally thick walls, a ditch cut into the rock on two sides and the steep rocky ridge on which it was built on the two other sides. In 1647, it was attacked by the Argyll government troops, but the Royalist Macleans resisted and drove the attackers away.

At the end of the 18th century, however, the Macleans surrendered Duart and all their other lands on Mull

Duart Castle stands on a rocky cliff overlooking the Sound of Mull

to the Duke of Argyll. Until 1751 the castle was inhabited by Hanoverian troops. It fell into ruins until the early 20th century, when Sir Fitzroy Donald Maclean bought and restored it.

WEIRD AND WONDERFUL

In c.1520, frustrated by his wife's inability to produce an heir, Lachlan Cattanach Maclean abandoned her on 'Lady's Rock', within sight of the castle, where she was drowned by the incoming tide.

BLAIR CASTLE

 LOCATION: Blair Atholl, Pitlochry, Perthshire PH18 5TL
DATE BUILT: (tower house) 1269
CASTLE STYLE: Tower House plus extensive additions
www.blair-castle.co.uk

Although today Blair Castle is an elegant, stately home, its origins are said to have started with a 13th century neighbours' dispute.

CUMMINGS' TOWER

In 1269, on his return to Scotland from a Crusade, David Murray, the Earl of Atholl, found that his neighbour, John I Comyn (also known as Cumming), Lord of Badenoch, had built a tower on his estate. Immediately, the earl complained to the king, who restored the estate to Murray.

The tower has always been the main element of Blair Castle, stronghold of the earls and dukes of Atholl ever since, although it is still known as 'Cummings' Tower'.

TWO SIEGES

When Mary Queen of Scots stayed at Blair Castle in 1540, the Atholl family had lived there for over 250 years. Previous family members had extended it considerably and over the following centuries, the simple tower house was adapted and enlarged to accommodate further Atholl family requirements.

During the English Civil War, Cromwell's forces besieged and captured the castle and in the second Jacobite Rising of 1745 and 1746, it was besieged again, this time by Jacobite forces. It was eventually reclaimed by its rightful owner, the second Duke of Atholl, who remodelled it as a Georgian mansion, replacing the turrets and crenellations with chimneys and sash windows.

 DID YOU KNOW?
Blair Castle currently provides the barracks for the Atholl Highlanders, the only legal private army in Europe.

Blair Castle has evolved into a grand mansion

SCOTTISH TOWERS

Although Scottish castle building began later than in England and Wales, it soon caught up and by the 13th century the castles being built in Scotland were almost identical to those south of the border.

Kilchurn Castle's ruins stand by Loch Awe in Argyll and Bute

DRAMATIC SITES

Across Britain, all castles were built to withstand attack and siege. At first, many important Scottish noblemen (who were often related to English noblemen through marriage) built castles resembling Edward I's constructions in the south. These castles were characterised by massive curtain walls, round towers and imposing gatehouses, although their sites were always far more dramatic than the English – such as Edinburgh (see p.70) or Dunnottar (see p.73).

CLAN CLASHES

By the middle of the 14th century, the Scottish nobility stopped building on such a grand scale and Scottish castle design began changing. Scottish lairds needed to protect themselves from attack

and instability as a succession of weak monarchies led to widespread feuding between rival clans. The border counties were also subject to raids by both the Scots and English during the Wars of Independence and for centuries after. While small fortified towers, or 'peles', were built around the border areas in northern England to protect local areas from these raids, the Scots began to build tower houses.

 DID YOU KNOW?
Scottish brochs and tower houses are sometimes confused. Both are tall, defensive towers but brochs were built during the Iron Age and are far more modest than tower houses, which were built from the early 15th century.

WEIRD AND WONDERFUL

Broch of Mousa, thought to have been built c.100BC, is the finest preserved example of a round tower in Shetland and the tallest still standing in the world.

TURRETS AND BATTLEMENTS

Rather than curtain walls and courtyards, the main parts of tower houses were their high, fortified towers with incredibly thick walls, battlemented parapets and strong corner turrets. Reaching up to five storeys high, with stone barrel-vaulted ceilings, these were self-contained structures filled with elegant rooms. Further protection was added outside with ditches, banks and extra walls called 'barmkins' surrounding the tower. With small doors on the ground floor, few tower houses had portcullises, instead, iron gates called 'yetts' provided protection.

DID YOU KNOW?

One reason tower houses became prevalent in Scotland was because wood was scarce. Wood was necessary for roofing and a tall, thin tower only required a small roof.

SELF-CONTAINED TOWERS

The main differences between the keeps of England and Wales and Scottish tower houses were that tower houses were self-contained. Everything the Scottish family needed was in the tower, while the English and Welsh castles were built with many rooms and facilities dotted around the bailey.

Another difference is that of location; while English and Welsh castles stood defiantly and conspicuously in the countryside, Scottish tower houses were usually built in mountainous or restricted areas, isolated and remote.

L-PLAN TOWERS

From the 13th to 17th centuries, L-plan towers were built as they gave inhabitants more space and a better chance of defending themselves from different angles.

By the 16th century, powerful nobles found it difficult to keep out of the political disorder of Britain, particularly in Scotland which continued to experience its own internal problems as well. This meant that tower houses continued to be built as symbols of authority and power and to protect their families.

By the mid-16th century, threats came more from petty raiders than from the assault of a full army and even in the 17th century, long after the English and Welsh had stopped building castles, Scottish lairds carried on building their tower houses and fortifying them as strongly as ever. They still called them castles, even when those who lived further south regarded the term as outdated.

IF YOU LIKED THIS...

Try visiting Castle Fraser, Alloa Tower or Clackmannan Tower.

DUNVEGAN CASTLE

LOCATION: Dunvegan, Isle of Skye IV55 8WF
DATE BUILT: c.1270
CASTLE STYLE: Originally a medieval tower house
www.dunvegancastle.com

The oldest continuously inhabited castle in Scotland, Dunvegan Castle on the Isle of Skye was built on high rocky cliffs. It has been the stronghold of the Chiefs of MacLeod for nearly eight centuries.

SON OF A KING

Parts of Dunvegan Castle date from the 9th century but the building of the current castle began in the 13th century. Dunvegan Castle was built in about 1270 on land inherited by Leod, a son of the king of the Isle of Man.

Leod constructed a stone fortification above the waters of Loch Dunvegan, with one entrance via the sea. Between 1340 and 1360, Malcolm, the third MacLeod chief, added thick curtain walls and a keep.

Dunvegan has been greatly remodelled over the centuries

THE FAIRY TOWER

The fairy tower was built around 1500 and houses the castle's most famous treasure: the fairy flag, a frail and faded piece of silk which was made some time between the fourth and seventh centuries. It is said to have been given to an early chief by his fairy wife. As the silk comes from the Middle East, some believe it to be the banner of Landoda, brought back from Constantinople in the 11th century by Harald Hardrada, an ancestor of Leod, although the fabric dates from four centuries before that. Whenever it is unfurled, the flag is said to bring victory to the MacLeods.

WEIRD AND WONDERFUL

Among its many powers, the fairy flag is said to be able to multiply MacLeod troops, save clansmen's lives, increase clanswomen's fertility and bring herring into Loch Dunvegan.

JEALOUS ASPIRATIONS

In the 15th century, Dunvegan was besieged by the MacDonalds, enemies of the MacLeods and in 1577 it was captured by Iain Dubh, a jealous uncle who (unsuccessfully) aspired to become chief.

CAWDOR CASTLE

LOCATION: Nairn IVI2 5RD
DATE BUILT: 1370
CASTLE STYLE: Tower house
www.cawdorcastle.com

Home to the Thanes of Cawdor, Cawdor Castle has had a violent history. Shakespeare linked the castle with Macbeth's killing of King Duncan, but it was not actually built until three centuries after Duncan's death.

LICENCE TO FORTIFY

The grey stone tower house of Cawdor Castle was built in approximately 1370. Turrets, crenellations and a curtain wall were added in 1454 after James II granted a licence to fortify the property.

Within two centuries, the tower house had been incorporated into a complex of additional buildings, including a ditch and drawbridge. The tower was built around a holly tree whose petrified remains are still in the basement.

SHAKESPEARE

Shakespeare used poetic licence with his play *Macbeth*, which he wrote in 1606. In the play, Macbeth and his wife murder King Duncan in nearby Inverness Castle, which is often confused with Cawdor Castle. In reality, Macbeth's men killed Duncan in battle and Macbeth took the Scottish throne. Cawdor Castle was not built for another 300 years.

KIDNAPPED!

In 1511, at the age of 12, Muriel Calder, the ninth Thane of Cawdor, was kidnapped and made to marry the Earl of Argyll's son, Sir John Campbell. After her death,

the inheritance of Cawdor Castle passed on to the Campbell family. By 1716, the castle was virtually abandoned, but a huge fire in 1819 prompted John Campbell, the first Earl Cawdor, to rebuild it.

 DID YOU KNOW?
Legend says that as kidnappers snatched Muriel Calder, her nurse branded her on the hip with a hot key so she could be identified if she was found again.

Cawdor Castle has been extended from its robust 14th century tower

URQUHART CASTLE

LOCATION: Drumnadrochit, Loch Ness IV63 6XJ

DATE BUILT: c.1400

CASTLE STYLE: Medieval tower house

www.historic-scotland.gov.uk

From its rocky position on the shores of Loch Ness, Urquhart Castle has faced much military action since it was first built in the early 13th century. Although now in ruins, it still dominates the area.

CHANGING HANDS

The earliest inhabitants of this site are believed to have been Picts, as in the sixth century Saint Columba visited the area to baptise a Pictish nobleman as he lay dying in his fort.

Located on the banks of Loch Ness Urquhart is one of the most dramatically sited Scottish castles

It is not known precisely when the present castle was built, but in 1229 Alexander II granted the Urquhart estate to Sir Thomas le Durward, whose son constructed a castle on the south of the headland, although building didn't start until the 13th century.

In 1296 Edward I captured the castle but it was recaptured by the Scots two years later. In 1308 Robert the Bruce took control and by 1329 Sir Robert Lauder had been put in charge, succeeded by his grandson Robert Chisholm in 1359. In 1395 the formidable MacDonald clan, the Lords of the Isles, seized the castle for themselves.

DOWNFALL

Eventually the MacDonalds' power was temporarily reduced and for about 35 years the Grants of Freuchie looked after the castle. The MacDonalds besieged it, twice taking control and destroying it at one point, but the Grants regained it and immediately refortified it with a great tower. In 1689, parts of the castle were blown up to prevent it from becoming a Jacobite stronghold.

DID YOU KNOW?

Local legend claims that the Loch Ness monster lives in underwater caves far below the ruins of Urquhart Castle. Many sightings have taken place there.

GLAMIS CASTLE

LOCATION: Angus, DD8 1RJ
DATE BUILT: 1400
CASTLE STYLE: L-plan tower house
www.glamis-castle.co.uk

In 1034 King Malcolm II was murdered at the Royal hunting lodge at Glamis. He was succeeded by his grandson Duncan, who was subsequently killed by Macbeth (another of Malcolm's grandsons).

MACBETH

Although Shakespeare wrote that Macbeth lived at Glamis, in real life he never did. In 1372 Robert II granted the site to his future son-in-law, Sir John Lyon, Thane of Glamis. The Lyon family, now Earls of Strathmore and Kinghorne, have owned the castle ever since. In about 1400, the second Earl of Strathmore and Kinghorne began building an L-plan tower house in place of the hunting lodge. The third earl, and first Lord Glamis, built the Great Tower in about 1435.

TREASON

The sixth Lord Glamis married Lady Janet Douglas. In 1528, Janet was accused of treason for bringing her father's supporters to Edinburgh. She was then charged with poisoning her husband who had died that year and in 1537, she was burned as a witch.

WEIRD AND WONDERFUL

One particular seat in the Glamis Castle chapel is always reserved for the 'Grey Lady', the ghost of the unfortunate Janet Douglas, said to inhabit the castle.

A GARRISON

During the Commonwealth of England, Scotland and Ireland, from 1653 to 1659, soldiers were stationed at Glamis. After that, major refurbishments were made to make it more comfortable. Glamis later became the childhood home of Elizabeth Bowes-Lyon, mother of Queen Elizabeth II.

IF YOU LIKED THIS...

Visit Cawdor Castle (p. 80) which has also been linked with the story of Macbeth.

Glamis Castle, said to be one of the most haunted castles in Britain

83

STIRLING CASTLE

LOCATION: Castle Esplanade, Stirling FK8 1EJ
DATE BUILT: c.11th century
CASTLE STYLE: Tower house and courtyard
www.stirlingcastle.gov.uk

There have been at least eight sieges of Stirling Castle, one of the most important castles in Scotland. Originally built in the 11th century, it was fought over fiercely by Edward I and William Wallace.

FIERCE FIGHTING

Standing 76 metres (250 feet) high on towering volcanic cliffs, Stirling Castle is strategically located by the River Forth, giving access to the Highlands, which made it important for anyone who wanted to rule Scotland. The first building of the 11th century was a wooden structure and this was what was fought over so violently by Edward I, William Wallace and Robert the Bruce in the late 13th and early 14th centuries. It has changed hands more often than any other Scottish castle.

DID YOU KNOW?

In 1304, Edward I besieged Stirling Castle with the largest trebuchet ever made. Called Warwolf, it took five master carpenters and 49 other labourers three months to make.

In 1296 Edward I seized the castle but Wallace recaptured it in 1297, losing it again in 1298 and retaking it in 1299. Edward I then ordered a large trebuchet (a siege engine, see p.95) and after three months of siege, the Scots surrendered Stirling and the English forces moved in for the following decade. The castle was recaptured in 1314 by Robert the Bruce's forces and its defences were partially destroyed to deter the English from reoccupying the castle.

SUMPTUOUS SURROUNDINGS

By 1336, during the second War of Scottish Independence, the English once more took control of Stirling Castle. While there, they undertook extensive building works. After a siege in 1341, the future Robert II of Scotland retook the castle and throughout the more peaceful 15th and 16th centuries, subsequent Scottish kings,

View from Stirling Castle over the surrounding countryside

Traditionally the strongest castle in Scotland, Stirling has changed hands more than any other

including James III, James IV and James V, completely renovated it.

Nothing remains of the earlier castle and almost all of the present buildings were constructed between 1490 and 1600, when it became central to the opulent courts of James IV, James V and James VI. The buildings they constructed display a varied mix of English, French and German styles. The Great Hall, for instance, is an example of one of the greatest Renaissance buildings in Britain.

WEIRD AND WONDERFUL

To celebrate the baptism of Prince Henry, the eldest son of James VI, in 1594, a full-sized ship was brought into the Great Hall and used to serve the food.

CORONATIONS AND BAPTISMS

In 1543, Mary Queen of Scots was crowned at Stirling and her son James was baptised there in 1566. Eight months later, James was crowned there after Mary had been forced to renounce the throne. Stirling became the base for James' supporters, while those who sided with Mary gathered at Edinburgh.

DID YOU KNOW?

Stirling's Great Hall features a dramatic hammerbeam ceiling, modelled on the ceiling of the Great Hall of Edinburgh Castle and does not contain a single nail.

LAST CONFLICTS

In the 17th century, following the restoration of the monarchy, Charles II became the last reigning sovereign to stay at Stirling Castle. Between 1708 and 1714, before the Jacobite Rebellions, the castle was refortified, which was well-timed as in 1746 Bonnie Prince Charlie besieged it – the castle's last encounter with war.

IF YOU LIKED THIS...

Visit Edinburgh Castle to see the ceiling of the Great Hall which inspired Stirling Castle's Great Hall.

Scotland

DOUNE CASTLE

LOCATION: Castle Road, Doune, Stirling FK16 6EA
DATE BUILT: c.1400
CASTLE STYLE: Tower house and courtyard
www.historic-scotland.gov.uk

In his 1814 novel *Waverley*, Sir Walter Scott described Doune Castle as a 'gloomy yet picturesque structure'. With its 'half-ruined turrets', the castle he referred to was built in the 14th century.

SCOTLAND'S UNCROWNED KING

It is likely that there was an ancient structure on the site of Doune Castle, as the name derives from the Gaelic word *dun*, meaning 'fort'.

The current castle was constructed in about 1398, when Robert Stewart, the Earl of Monteith and Fife, became the Duke of Albany. He was the Regent of Scotland from 1388 until his death in 1420.

DID YOU KNOW?
The Duke of Albany was the son of Robert II and the brother of Robert III. He remained in the centre of Scottish politics for around 50 years.

Throughout that time the Regent was the most intimidating man in Scotland and Doune was virtually a royal castle. Its most striking features are the great gatehouse and hall. Unusually, it was hardly extended in later years. On Albany's death, the castle passed to his son who was executed within five years and the castle passed to the Crown.

Doune is one of the best preserved medieval castles in Scotland

THE EARLS OF MORAY

In the 16th century, Margaret Tudor's brother-in-law was made Captain of Doune Castle. His son was created Lord Doune and his grandson became the Earl of Moray through marriage. Subsequent Earls of Moray owned Doune Castle until the 20th century. During the Jacobite Rising of 1745, the castle was occupied by Bonnie Prince Charlie and several government soldiers were imprisoned there. The castle gradually fell out of use, but in 1883 it was substantially restored.

KILCHURN CASTLE

LOCATION: North east end of Loch Awe, Dalmally PA33 1AJ
DATE BUILT: 1450
CASTLE STYLE: Tower house and courtyard
www.historic-scotland.gov.uk

Built on a small island in the mid-15th century, Kilchurn Castle was only accessible by water for most of its existence. After much remodelling and changes of hands, it was destroyed by lightning in 1760.

FIVE STOREY TOWER

In 1450 Sir Colin Campbell, first Lord of Glenorchy, built a five storey tower house with a courtyard and barmkin on a tiny island at the end of Loch Awe in the west of Scotland.

Within 100 years, additional buildings including a hall and round corner towers had been added and further buildings were erected in the 16th and 17th centuries. Eventually, the castle practically covered the whole island.

Through marriage the MacGregor clan were related to the Campbells and at the end of the 15th century the MacGregors were appointed as Keepers of Kilchurn. During the early years of the 17th century however, there was a violent feud between the two clans and the Campbells retook the castle.

GOVERNMENT GARRISON

In 1681, Sir John Campbell of Glenorchy became the first Earl of Breadalbane

and began refortifying the castle, adding military quarters that could accommodate 200 troops. During the 1715 and 1745

Kilchurn was abandoned in the middle of the 18th century

Jacobite Risings, these barracks were used by government forces, but within 15 years, the castle was struck by lightning and was subsequently abandoned.

In 1817, the water level of Loch Awe was lowered, enabling direct access to the castle by road.

IF YOU LIKED THIS...
Try visiting Castle Campbell in central Scotland, which was also owned by Sir Colin Campbell in the 15th century.

Scotland

CULZEAN CASTLE

LOCATION: Maybole, Ayrshire KA19 8LE
DATE BUILT: c.1590
CASTLE STYLE: Georgian mansion built around a tower house
www.culzeanexperience.org

Although there are records of a tower house at Culzean in the 15th century, the established history of the current castle began a century later. By the 17th century, it was a comfortable family home.

THE HOUSE OF COVE

In the earliest written records, Culzean Castle was known as 'Coif Castle' or the 'House of Cove', as it was built on a sheer rock face above a network of caves. In the 17th century, the name changed to 'Cullean Castle' and the spelling became Culzean sometime over the next 100 years, although it is still pronounced 'Cullane'.

In 1569, the fourth Earl of Cassilis gave his brother, Sir Thomas Kennedy, the estates at Culzean. Sir Thomas began building

and enlarging the tower house during the 1590s but it was not the Kennedy family's most important property until 1759. When David Kennedy, 10th Earl of Cassilis inherited the estate, he commissioned the architect Robert Adam to rebuild the earlier castle.

HUGE ROUND TOWER

Between 1777 and 1792, Adam transformed the old fortified tower house into a classical Georgian mansion, with medieval style embellishments including turrets, towers and crenellations. On its north side, directly and dramatically on the edge of the cliff, there is a huge round tower made up of large circular rooms and a magnificent oval staircase – considered to be among Adam's finest and most interesting work.

DID YOU KNOW?

In 1945 Dwight D. Eisenhower, the 34th President of the United States, was given the tenancy of a flat on the top floor of Culzean Castle, in thanks for America's support during the Second World War.

Culzean is both a cliff-edged castle and an elegant mansion

BRAEMAR CASTLE

LOCATION: Braemar AB35 5XR
DATE BUILT: 1628
CASTLE STYLE: L-plan tower house
www.braemarcastle.co.uk

Standing high above the River Dee, Braemar Castle was originally built in the 17th century as a hunting lodge by one of Scotland's most powerful noblemen.

RULERS OF DEESIDE
In 1628, John Erskine, Earl of Mar built the first tower of Braemar Castle as an L-plan tower house. He said it was a hunting lodge, but its real purpose was more likely to be a way to restrict the growing power of the Farquharson clan.

For centuries, the Earls of Mar had been asserting themselves as rulers of Deeside, the area around Braemar, and the feuds between their clan and the Farquharsons showed no sign of lessening.

WEIRD AND WONDERFUL
There have been sightings of several ghosts in Braemar Castle, including a young woman, a piper and the 'Black Colonel'.

THE FARQUHARSONS
During the rebellions leading up to the Jacobite Risings, Braemar Castle was used as an important garrison. John Farquharson, known as the 'Black Colonel', attacked and burned it and it was left in ruins for 60 years. The Earls of Mar never lived there again.

Braemar Castle has an unusual star-shaped curtain wall

In 1732, none other than John Farquharson, ninth Laird of Invercauld, bought the ruin and surrounding lands, but realising that the Jacobite cause was lost, he leased it to the Hanoverian government for use as a barracks. Restorations began in 1748, with a zigzag encircling rampart and crenellations added to the originally conical turrets. In 1807, the castle was returned to the Farquharsons who made it their family home.

IF YOU LIKED THIS...
You'll like Corgarff Castle, also in Aberdeenshire.

FLOORS CASTLE

LOCATION: Kelso, Roxburghshire TD5 7SF
DATE BUILT: 1721
CASTLE STYLE: Symmetrical Georgian country house
www.roxburghe.net

Standing on the River Tweed close to the Cheviot Hills, Floors is the largest inhabited castle in Scotland. Built as a Georgian country house around an existing tower house, it contrasts strongly with fortified castles.

BUILT FOR ELEGANCE

In 1721 William Adam, the leading Scottish architect of the time, was commissioned by the first Duke of Roxburghe to create a large house on the site of an old tower house. With elegantly symmetrical wings and large windows, Floors Castle was never built for defence.

BORDER REIVERS

From the late 13th to the early 17th centuries, the border lands between Scotland and England, also known as Marches, were a dangerous area, with frequent raids, attacks and counterattacks from gangs of Reivers (raiders). Coming from both Scottish and English families, Reivers raided estates on the borders of both countries. 'Border Law' was developed, giving victims the right to mount a counter-raid. March Wardens were appointed to maintain justice, but they were ineffectual as many Wardens were Reivers themselves. In 1603, when James VI of Scotland became James I of England, he began unifying the two countries. The March Wardens were disbanded and wanted men were caught and executed.

Floors was always more of a country house than a fortress

By the time Floors was built, there was no longer any need for strong fortifications and in the 19th century, the sixth Duke of Roxburghe employed Scotland's foremost architect, William Playfair, to modify the building in the ornamental style fashionable at the time.

 **WEIRD AND WONDERFUL**

A holly tree marks the spot where James II was killed while besieging the castle in 1460, when his own cannon exploded.

BALMORAL CASTLE

 LOCATION: Ballater, Aberdeenshire AB35 5TB
DATE BUILT: (original) 1390, (current) 1852–56
CASTLE STYLE: Scottish Baronial
www.balmoralcastle.com

'My dear paradise in the Highlands' was Queen Victoria's description of Balmoral Castle. Rebuilt for her and Prince Albert in the mid-19th century, it has served as the royal family's holiday home ever since.

'BOUCHMORALE'

In 1390, Sir William Drummond built a large house in the country by the River Dee, known as 'Bouchmorale'. It was rented by the second son of the first Earl of Huntly in the 15th century and 200 years later, it passed to the Farquharson family. By 1830, Sir Robert Gordon acquired a lease for the castle and made major modifications.

FREEDOM AND PEACE

Queen Victoria and Prince Albert rented Balmoral in 1848 and bought it three years later. Victoria found the house 'small but pretty' and wrote that 'all seemed to breathe freedom and peace and to make one forget the world and its sad turmoils'.

 DID YOU KNOW?
Queen Victoria commissioned several artists to stay at Balmoral and record it in paintings, including the Landseer brothers, William Wyld, Carl Haag and William Henry Fisk.

HOLIDAY HOME

Although he employed an architect, Prince Albert took a close interest in the designs of their new castle, which was built in the Scottish Baronial style. By 1856, the royal couple moved in and the old castle was demolished. Victoria and Albert took great interest in their staff, setting up a lending library and turning the surrounding land into a working estate.

Balmoral Castle is built from granite quarried on the estate

GLOSSARY

ARROW SLITS
Thin vertical openings in castle walls through which archers can launch arrows.

BALLISTA
A medieval catapult used for hurling large stones.

BARBICAN
The outer defence of a castle, typically a double tower above a gate or drawbridge. Good examples are at Chepstow (see p.47) and Leeds Castle (see p.23).

BARMKINS
Defensive enclosures, usually around smaller castles, tower houses or pele towers, in Scotland and northern England. Kilchum Castle (see p.87) was developed within a barmkin.

BASTIDES
Fortified new towns built in Languedoc, Gascony and Aquitaine during the 13th and 14th centuries.

BATTERING RAM
A long, heavy bar used to break doors down.

BATTLEMENTS
Parapets on castle walls with regular indentations.

BURGHS
Boroughs or chartered towns in Scotland, such as Aberdeen and Perth.

CELTS
An intelligent and enterprising race of people originally based in central Europe who spread to western Europe and the British Isles.

CLAN
A group of families descending from a common ancestor; an important social unit in Scotland.

CONCENTRIC CASTLES
Castles with two or more surrounding curtain walls with a lower outer wall, such as the Tower of London (see p.16), Caerphilly (see p.54) and Beaumaris Castles (see p.64).

CONSTABLE
The governor of a royal castle.

CRENELLATIONS
Another word for battlements.

CURTAIN WALLS
Walls built around a castle.

DONJON
A great tower; Warwick Castle (see p.31) features two towers that were built in the style of the French Donjon.

DRAWBRIDGE
A wooden bridge that was raised or lowered across a moat.

DRUM TOWERS
Large, wide, circular towers; the large drum towers at Beaumaris Castle (see p.64) are good examples.

ENCLOSURE
An area enclosed by a fence or wall.

FEUDAL SYSTEM
An economic and political system of the Middle Ages in which land was held in return for services, guaranteed by oaths of loyalty.

FIEFS
Areas of land, usually given on condition of feudal service.

FREEMEN
People who were not slaves, but had rights and privileges like other citizens.

GUN PORTS
Openings in castle walls which guns or cannons could be pushed through for firing.

JACOBITE
A supporter of the deposed James VII of Scotland, II of England and his descendants in their claim to the British throne after the Revolution of 1688.

JUSTICIAR
From the 11th century to the end of the 13th century in both England and Scotland, the Justiciar was the chief political and legal officer who stood in for the king in his absence.

KEEP
The main tower within the walls of a medieval castle, such as the White Tower at the Tower of London (see p.16).

KNIGHTS
High ranking soldiers of the Middle Ages.

L-PLAN
A castle or tower house in the shape of an 'L', characteristically built in the 13th to 17th centuries, mainly in Scotland, but also sometimes in England.

MACHICOLATIONS
Projecting parapets on castles with openings through which stones, sand, boiling water or boiling oil could be dropped on enemies. Bodiam Castle (see p.25) features some prominent machicolations.

MANGONEL
A device for throwing stones and other heavy missiles.

MARCHER LORDS
Trusted nobles appointed by the king of England to guard the border between England and Wales.

MARCHES
The border areas between England and Wales and England and Scotland where constant feuds occurred during the 13th to 16th centuries.

MEDIEVAL
A term referring to the fifth to 15th centuries in Europe, also called the Middle Ages.

MOAT
A deep, wide ditch usually surrounding a castle or town.

MOTTE AND BAILEY

A type of castle built on a raised earthwork mound (motte) and surrounded by a protective fence (bailey). Carisbrooke (p.22) and Totnes Castles (p.28) are good examples.

NORMAN

The conquerors of Britain in 1066 and their descendants who originally came from Normandy. Also refers to their style of castle building.

PALISADES

Defensive fences usually made of timber. No original palisades exist, but there is a fine model at Mountfichet Castle in Essex.

PARAPETS

Low protective walls or ramparts around the edge of castle roofs to protect or conceal defenders. St Mawes Castle (p.29) has a good example of a parapet.

PELES

Small tower houses. There are good examples at Corbridge and Elsdon in Northumberland.

PICTS

An ancient group of people living in Scotland of uncertain origins who adopted the Celtic way of life. Their name comes from the Latin word for 'painted people'.

PORTCULLIS

A heavy iron or wood gate made of bars or slats, suspended in the gateway of a castle and lowered to prevent enemies passing through. Edinburgh Castle (p.70) still has a working portcullis.

POSTERN GATE

A secondary castle door or gate, often hidden or at the rear of a castle. Denbigh Castle (p.59) has a good example of a postern gate.

RAMPARTS

Defensive walls of castles or walled cities that are broad at the top with walkways and usually a stone parapet. Warwick Castle (p.31) has strong ramparts.

REIVERS

English and Scottish raiders along the Anglo-Scottish border who did not care about victims' nationalities. Reivers terrorised the borders for nearly 300 years, from the late 13th century to the mid-16th century.

RETAINER

A supporter of a person of rank such as a nobleman or a king in England.

SCOTTISH BARONIAL

A 19th century design style that drew on stylistic elements from Scottish tower houses and castles, including battlements, machicolations and parapets. Balmoral Castle (p.91) is a fine example of this style.

SERFS

Members of the lowest feudal class attached to land owned by a lord and required to work in return for certain rights. Serfs were not allowed to move or work elsewhere.

SHELL KEEPS

Circular stone towers on top of mottes. Lewes (p.15), Carisbrooke (p.22) and Lincoln Castles (p.32) have shell keeps.

SIEGE

An attack on a city or castle in which the attackers cut off supplies and access to the castle with the goal of conquering the inhabitants.

SLIGHT

To order the destruction of a castle. Dunbar, for example, was slighted and then refortified.

SQUARE KEEPS

Square-shaped central towers of stone castles. Dover Castle (p.13) has a square keep.

THANE

A medieval man, ranking between a freeman and a hereditary noble, who held land granted by the king.

TOWER HOUSE

A particular type of small castle either consisting only of a single tower or with a tower as the main aspect of the building.

TRACERY

Ornamental interlaced patterns, particularly on Gothic windows as in Tattershall (p.37) and Cholmondeley Castles.

TRAITORS' GATE

Built by Edward I as a water entrance to the Tower of London (p.16), many Tudor prisoners later entered through the same gate which was then known as Traitors' Gate.

TREBUCHET

A medieval machine used for hurling large stones or other missiles in siege warfare.

VASSAL

A person who was granted the use of land from a feudal lord and received protection in return for homage and allegiance.

VILLEINS

Feudal tenants who were bound to serve their masters like serfs but they also enjoyed some of the rights of freemen.

WARD (OR BAILEY)

A courtyard or open area in a castle enclosed by a curtain wall, such as at Caerphilly (p.54) and Conwy Castles (p.62).

WATTLE-AND-DAUB

Building material of interwoven twigs plastered together with mud or clay, used to infill timber-framed walls.

YETTS

Iron gates that protect castle entrances.

USEFUL SOURCES

WEBSITES

www.britishcastle.co.uk
www.bbc.co.uk/history/british
www.castlexplorer.co.uk
www.english-heritage.org.uk
www.nationaltrust.org.uk
www.royal.gov.uk
www.britroyals.com
www.royalcollection.org.uk

BOOKS

Ivanhoe, Sir Walter Scott (1819), (Penguin Classics, 2003)

English Castles: A Guide by Counties, A A Pettifer (Boydell Press, 2002)

Allen Brown's English Castles, R Allen Brown (Boydell Press, 2004)

AA Best of Britain's Castles: 100 of the Most Impressive Historic Sites in Britain (AA Publishing, 2004)

Castles: England, Scotland, Ireland, Wales, Plantagenet Somerset Fry (David & Charles, 2005)

Castles in Context: Power, Symbolism and Landscape, 1066 to 1500, Robert Liddiard (Windgather Press, 2005)

Castles from the Air: An Aerial View of Britain's Finest Castles, Paul Johnson, Adrian Warren and Dae Sasitorn (Bloomsbury Press, 2006)

The Rise of the Castle, M W Thompson (Cambridge University Press, 2008)

FILMS AND TELEVISION

Mary Queen of Scots (1971): film featuring Alnwick Castle, with Vanessa Redgrave and Glenda Jackson

Macbeth (1971): Roman Polanski film, featuring Lindisfarne and Bamburgh Castles

Monty Python and the Holy Grail (1974): film featuring Doune Castle

Tempest (1979): film directed by Derek Jarman, featuring Bamburgh Castle

Ivanhoe (1982): film adaptation of Sir Walter Scott's novel, featuring Doune Castle, with Anthony Andrews

Sword of the Valiant: the Legend of Sir Gawain and the Green Knight (1984): film with Miles O'Keeffe and Sean Connery, featuring Cardiff Castle

Highlander (1986): film with Sean Connery and Christopher Lambert, featuring Eilean Donan Castle

Robin Hood, Prince of Thieves (1991): film featuring Alnwick Castle and others, starring Kevin Costner

Elizabeth (1998): film featuring Alnwick Castle, with Cate Blanchett

Harry Potter and the Philosopher's Stone (2001): film featuring Alnwick Castle, with Daniel Radcliffe

The Virgin Queen (2005): series of four BBC documentaries, featuring Alnwick, Chillingham, Raby and Warkworth Castles

The Queen (2006): film featuring Balmoral Castle, Castle Fraser, Blairquhan Castle and Culzean Castle, starring Helen Mirren